THE REBBE'S ADVICE

THE REBBE'S ADVICE

volume 2

adapted by
Rabbi Chaim Dalfin

MENDELSOHN PRESS

New York

The Rebbe's Advice
volume 2
Rabbi Chaim Dalfin

Copyright 1998 © Mendelsohn Press
All Rights Reserved.

No part of this book may be used or reproduced in any form without written permission from the publisher, except for brief quotations in reviews.

Request for information or additional books
should be addressed to:

Mendelsohn Press
390A Kingston Ave. Brooklyn, N.Y. 11225
Tel. (718) 467-1957

ISBN: 1-880-880-25-3
First Edition Spring 1998

Printed in the United States of America

Design by Mendelsohn Press• Brooklyn, N.Y (718) 735-7448
Printing by Moriah Offset•Brooklyn, N.Y. (718) 693-3800

In Honor of the Lubavitcher Rebbe

May it be Hashem's Will that all brochos be openly revealed as good and that our Rebbe derive abundant nachas from his shluchim, his chasidim as well as from all Israel.

May Hashem arouse "all those that repose in the dust" and restore all souls back in physical bodies so that the entire Jewish Nation may be speedily taken to the Holy Land, with the coming of our righteous Moshiach.

In honor of the 1st Yartzeit of
Malka Miriam (Donna) Schaeffer

The Schaeffer Family:

Leib Avrohom, his wife Chaya Bayla

and their children

Chana Rochel, Mushka and Malka Miriam

as well as the extended Schaeffer and Siegel families

They should all live long, blessed, good years.

TABLE OF CONTENTS

Dedication

Acknowledgements

Introduction

1
CLOTHING AND APPEARANCE

Each day new garment 1

Wearing the same *sirtug* (chasidic frock) for 120 years 1

Clean clothing 2

Polishing the shoes 2

Right over left 3

Single Breasted Suit 3

Increasing *parnasa* 4

Beard and *peyos* 4

Color of *shabbos* clothing 4

Silk garment on *shabbos* and *yom tov* 5

Girls dressing up as boys 5

Men wearing rings 5

Black hat 6

Schochet wearing long coat 6

Modern clothing for *shidduch* purposes 7

Protection from bad friends 7
Wearing suit for rabbinic audition 8
Women's modest dress 8
Tznius and Moshiach 9
Dresses and shorts 9
Shliach needs two pairs of shoes and *kapotes* 10

2

TORAH CLASSES, KOLLEL

Chapter 41 in *Tanya* a Remedy for problems 11
Must get paid 12
Kabbalah lectures 12
Enthusiasm for Kolel 13
Returning to *kollel* after long interval 13
Kollel is made for mature, responsible adults 13
Can a Jew who converted to Christianity join a Torah study group? 14
Mixed Torah classes 16
Learning in a yeshiva 17
Preventing girl from living with mother who lives with non-Jew 18
Studying Kabbalah 18
Learning *sichos* in bed 18

3
CHINUCH, EDUCATION

Do not forget your days in *Tomchei Temimim* 21
Staying home 21
Giving prizes 22
Hospital a place for outreach 22
Leaving yeshiva to learn a trade 22
Benefit of school tests 23
Getting children to listen 24
Once a *Tomim*, always a *Tomim* 24
Students who ask questions but don't want answers 24
Thanksgiving offering - increasing Torah and *mitzvos* 25
Chabad *korbon todah* 25
Tehillim blesses the month 26
Authentic commentary 26
Understanding what you are reading 26

4
HEALTH AND MEDICINE

Overweight 29
Cure for heart attacks 29
Give a *kiddush* on *Simchas Torah* 30
Autistic children 31

Remedy for relaxation 31
Bitter and sweet pills 31
Stay away from hypnosis 32
Auspices of Jewish Meditation Institute 32
Schizophrenia 33
Hospital is a place for healers 34
Cancer "that" illness 34

5

TZEDAKA

Hiskashrus 35
Guards from evil eye 36
Curing foot aches contributing
to educational institutions 36
Give *tzedaka* before visiting
the doctor 37
Reducing real estate problems 37
Business venture going sour 38
Remedy for *bitochan* 39
Having male children 39
Bikur cholim fund 40
Tithing from future revenues 40
Diminishing *tzedaka* because of decrease in income ... 41
Tzedaka when business is
not successful 42
Give half now 42

Not contributing to questionable organizations 43
Dedicating *seforim* 44
Extra money in a fund 45
Deeding a property to a yeshiva 45
Flood 46

6

SHIDDUCHIM, BRIDE AND GROOM, PREGNANCY

Two Marriage choices 47
Consulting parents 47
Money 47
Sooner than later 48
Husband and wife should learn together 48
Good offer, but I have no job 48
Substitution for *yechidus* 49
When to ask for *brocha* about healthy pregnancy 49
Going to the *mikva* during the ninth month of pregnancy . . .50
Parents may know about pregnancy before five months 50
Husband should not be in the delivery room 50
Say chapters of *Tehillim* during the delivery 51
Delaying *chasuna* leads to breakdown in *tznius* 51

7

JEWISH NAMES

Channels personal energy 53

Name, job, and character 53

Who decides a child's name 54

Parents should agree 54

Do not mix in 54

I had that in mind 55

Name a girl at first chance 55

Baby naming before bris 56

The name Avrohom 56

Naming after a living person 57

The names of the Previous Rebbe and Tzemach Tzedek 57

Combining names: Yes or no? 57

Name makes you responsible 58

The meaning of Chaya Mushka 58

Changing names 59

The name to counter cancer 60

Changing name chosen by grandparent 60

Reverting to a previous name 60

Calling yourself by Hebrew name 61

The name Marta 61

The names Collete, Algeria, Duna 61

Rebbe's suggested names 62

Names of *goyim* 63

Name after one who died in war 63

Remedy for long life 63

Order of names 64
Publicizing author's and contributors' names 64
Whispering Rebbe's name into ear 65

8
BUSINESS, OCCUPATIONS, INVESTMENTS

Picture your Rebbe's face 67
Pushka's in business 68
Closing business Friday after midday 68
Profits of *Shabbos* to non-observant partner 68
Business partners get it in writing 69
Horse trainer 69
Horse betting 70
Not being partner in business if not knowledgeable 70
Journalist 71
No such thing as a "professional" *chasid* 71
Investing in Israel 72
What is a Chabad Rebbe's job? 72

9
MITZVOS AND JEWISH CUSTOMS

Kiddush Levana sanctification of the moon 73
Soldiers wearing ammunition on *Shabbos* 74
Eating carob on *Lag b'Omer* 74

Immersing in the *mikva* before visiting the cemetery 75

Chazan should review, yearly, the meaning of the words 75

Forgot to *daven* 76

Torah that fell 76

Tikun for having child from gentile 76

Gentile might have touched wine 77

Afraid *Upsherinish* will cause cold 77

Upsherinish customs 78

Make *chasidisher* farbrengen at Bar-Mitzvah 79

Bar-Mitzvah trip 80

Celebrating a deceased child's birthday 80

Chasidic Bas-Mitzvah celebration 81

Tikun for forgetting to put on Rabbeinu Tam's *Tefillin* *81*

Tikun for lighting *Shabbos* candles late 81

Tikunim for disgracing *shul* and *Sefer Torah* 82

Melave Malka or *Mesibas Shabbos* as Bas-Mitzvah celebration .83

Birthday customs and practices 84

Birthday celebration for one-year-old 85

Cornerstone ceremony 86

Reciting *ma'amor* at *chanukas habayis* 87

Sleeping with *tzitzis* 87

Kissing the *mezuzah* at night 87

Stopping the pulling of hairs from beard 88

Kashrus standards Benedictine brand 88

Overdoing grief 89

10
MISCELLANEOUS

Dream interpretation 91
Who is an authentic dream interpreter? 91
Moving into home during *chodesh Elul* 92
Moving on a Tuesday 92
Who are truly *yididim u'mevinim*? 93
Happy birthday 93
No such thing as "I am not a Reform, Conservative, or Orthodox Jew" 93
Jewish unity or division 94
Do not curse gentiles 95
No burden for the Rebbe 95
Loneliness 96
Leaving Israel 96
No reality to "magic" 96
Traveling legally 96
Olympics is *avoda zora* 97
Holocaust memorials 97
Converts 99
Homesick and yearning 99
Passing away with holiness 99
Non-Jew's fulfillment 102
Abusing saying "*l'chayim*" 103

Transforming "Transcendental Meditation" into
Jewish Meditation 104

Souvenirs from Israel 107

Relating to afterlife 107

Dual realities: Life and death 108

Daily relationship with departed soul 110

Explanation for unexpected passing of young child 111

Salt: removing the negative energy 112

How to get out of prison 113

Looking at the Rebbe's picture 114

Do not avoid a *Din Torah* *114*

I do not take responsibility for what is said in my name .114

There are no "*misnagdim*" today 115

Say *Tfilas HaDerech* daily during a trip 115

Safety measures for car trips 115

Doing *mivtzoyim* on trips 116

Shabbos entrance tickets 116

Swimming 116

Charms, amulets 117

EPILOGUE

GLOSSARY

PUBLISHERS PREFACE

Countless people from all walks of life, regardless of their background or profession, consulted with the Rebbe with regard to a wide range of personal problems. Whether the issue involved was spiritual, marital, financial, medical or another, the Rebbe's advice was always sought after.

Shortly before his passing, the Rebbe Rashab said,"I am going to heaven, and the Kesavim (his Torah Teachings) I leave for you (for the Lubavitcher Chasidim). The Rebbe lives forever through his teachings, and as our Sages teach us "more so now than before."

The Rebbe's teachings are generally divided into four categories.

1. Sichos and Mamorim, which are talks and discourses elucidating different areas in Torah.

2. Rishimos, personal writings and recollections, which he compiled during the 30 year period from his wedding until after he ascended to the leadership of Chabad.

3. Yechidus, oral advice given during private audiences.

4. Igros Kodesh, correspondence addressed to private individuals, politicians, public people etc.

The latter form of instruction entails a collection of some 200,000 letters on a varied and colorful array of subjects.

In the late 1980's the Rebbe ordered the publication of these letters. They were arranged according to the date of their writing, with some twenty-four volumes until the year 1965 alone. Many letters were not included in the series, which represents a fraction of all those transcribed in that period. The Rebbe steadily demanded that the publication of these letters be executed as fast as was humanly possible and constantly asked his secretariat if the Chasidim were availing themselves of the directives contained therein. It is interesting that this directive to publish the Igros Kodesh (the books containing the Rebbe's letters) came in the last few years before the Rebbe suffered a stroke which impaired the Rebbe's communication with the Chasidim.

Nowadays also, although the Rebbe is not here physically to teach, direct and guide us, we still have his many letters which contain clear, concise instruction for many of life's problems. Today, thousands of Jews turn to these letters to seek advice in resolving their daily uncertainties. They write a letter to the Rebbe, which they put into Igros Kodesh. Whatever letter the Igros Kodesh opens to they take to their Rav for clarification. The Rav instructs them in how to apply the answer to their day to day life.

In Sefer HaSichos 5749, volume 2, page 489, which was edited by the Rebbe, he writes, ". . . the necessity of a lottery in day-to-day life is, when a person cannot decide what direction to follow in general matters of life . . ., they would make a lottery, and would act according to the results of the lottery, since it is G-d's Will . . .

"As is known the ancient Jewish Custom, when one needs to decide how to conduct himself in practical life (where Torah does not explicitly give instructions) one would make a lottery by opening up a Torah Book, Chumash etc. The particular verse where the Torah Book opens to—which is Divine Providence—would be the resolve to his query. The verse would be a sign that G-d wants him to conduct himself this way."

Many stories abound of incredible miracles resulting directly through compliance with the Rebbe's directions.

The following story clearly illustrates this method of communication with the Rebbe:

In March of 1997 a family living in Israel was involved in a horrific car accident. The father was rushed to a hospital in Teberias where he lay in critical condition, attended to by the best doctors in the facility. His wife and children stayed nearby with a Chasidic family who tried their best to comfort the distraught woman. "I have twelve children!" she cried hysterically. "How can he be taken from us?" She beseeched the couple to ask the Rebbe for his blessing and the Chosid consulted a volume of the Rebbe's letters. The words sprang out of the page: "A change in place brings a change of fortune."

The Chosid was somewhat astonished. Of what relevance was this to the current situation? He consulted with the book once more, this time receiving an answer "[to consult with] an expert doctor for success both physically and spiritually." Armed with this directive, he immediately began contacting the biggest doctors in the country. The patient had meanwhile contracted pneumonia and had been infected by a microbe in his bloodstream. His situation was grave.

A team of professional doctors arrived to examine the patient, and they deemed his treatment inappropriate. "He must change locations," they instructed, and the words of the Rebbe suddenly became startlingly clear. That afternoon he was transferred, his medication changed, and the doctor's prognosis called for some damage to the brain upon recovery. When the patients wife mentioned the Rebbe's blessing, the doctor shook his head in amazement. "I wish we could be so optimistic!" he said.

Within ten days the patient was sitting up in a chair unassisted, hearing and talking as normal. The outcome had completely shattered the expected prognosis.

It is our fervent hope that the publication of this book will fulfill the Rebbe's directive to our publishing company, that "it should be a great success in the spreading of the wellsprings outside." May this dissemination of the Rebbe's advice hasten the Redemption, when we will merit to hear "the New Torah from the mouth of Moshiach," speedily in our days.

Mendelsohn Press
Aaron Mendelsohn
11 Nissan, 5758

ACKNOWLEDGEMENTS

With much gratitude to Hashem, the first volume of The Rebbe's Advice has been received warmly by people throughout the world. The many telephone calls received, expressing satisfaction and desire for more of the Rebbe's advice, prompted us to present a second volume. This volume focuses on some new topics not included in the first volume-such as Jewish names and Tzinus, (modesty in dress) for men and women. We look forward to your comments and suggestions.

When it comes to thanking people for their assistance, one realizes how insufficient thanks really are. Anything one can say will only express a glimpse of the heart's true feelings. To all those who gave of themselves to help spread the ideals of Torah and *mitzvos*, the true thanks will come from the Al-mighty G-d, Who is limitless and infinite. It is G-d who truly 'pays back' with tangible blessings.

To begin with, I give thanks to G-d, who granted me the strength to persevere in this work. G-d gives strength in any endeavor. All that G-d asks is that we allow His blessings to enter. Fortunate are those who make themselves a vessel to receive His blessings and who acknowledge that it comes from Him.

For each person who assisted in the book becoming a reality, I wish that G-d's blessing be bestowed upon him and his family. I would like to specially recognize several people for their generous assistance.

First, I would like to thank our dear and beloved Rebbe, Rabbi M. M. Schneerson, whose teachings and directives are alive now, more than before. The Rebbe did not just leave us a legacy; he lives on through the study and practice of his teachings, which I share with you in this book.

Special thanks go to my parents, Reb Aron Hillel and Miriam Dalfin, who gave me my educational foundation and continue to strengthen it; my dear wife Bashi; my five children, Menachem Mendel, Shterna Sara, Brocha, Hinda Fraida and Chaya Mushka, who constantly kept me on my feet, making the combination of writing and family responsibilities a real challenge; my uncle Yaccov and his wife Yehudit who live in Costa Rica and continue to support my projects; and my brother Anshel who continues to support my endeavors. I thank my paternal grandparents of blessed memory, Reb Shlomo and Baila Dalfin, and my maternal grandparents of blessed memory, Reb Shlomo Menashe and Hinda Fraida Wiroslow, who survived the Holocaust and were living examples of faith in G-d and Torah. May this book contribute to the eternal bliss that they experience in the world of truth.

I want to express my appreciation to Mr. Bryan Ellison, who realized the potential of the manuscript and made it a reality by editing the book, and a special thank you to my publisher Aaron Mendelsohn of Mendelsohn Press. Finally, I thank all those whose names I may have missed. May each of you be blessed.

May this book be received and viewed as a stepping stone toward the fulfillment of Moshiach's response to the Baal Shem Tov: "(I will come) when your wellsprings will be spread to the outside world." Amen, may it be now!

INTRODUCTION

"Words of *tzaddikim* are eternal."

An American businessperson who owned a lumber company once came to seek Rabbi Yosef Yitzchok Schneerson's advice. The Rebbe offered his suggestions, and went on to encourage him to increase his observance of Torah and *mitzvos*. Startled, the businessperson responded to the Rebbe, "I did not ask you about my spirituality; I asked you about improving my business so that I can make more money."

The Rebbe answered, "Just the opposite. Business issues are *your* expertise; I have no association with them. Yet, you seek my advice! On the other hand, Torah and *mitzvos*, which are my primary 'business' and the business of my fathers and grandfathers: that you do *not* inquire of me."

The story has a profound moral. What is the purpose of writing a book on the Rebbe's advice concerning issues that are not really a Rebbe's expertise? It may be true that personal issues of business, health, marriage, and investment are not a Rebbe's expertise, but Torah and *mitzvos* are. Since a Rebbe has been given a special gift from G-d to communicate what the Torah says about these issues, he connects us to the essence of each issue. If one thinks that a Rebbe is one who has expertise in stocks, real estate, medicine, and other day-to-day issues, let him think again. That would be a big mistake. (See my book *To Be Chasidic*, chapter 21, J. Aronson, 1996)

The Lubavitcher Rebbe, Rabbi Menachem Mendel Schneerson, has imbued world Jewry with words of wisdom, advice and meaning. The Rebbe's advice has been addressed to all kinds of problems, literally helping thousands of people. This illustrious *tzaddik* has dealt with problems and issues ranging from health to finance, from birth to marriage, and from theology to psychology.

All of us need individualized advice at certain times. The Rebbe provides this. You might ask, how is his advice different than consulting your local rabbi or counselor? The uniqueness of the Rebbe's guidance lies in his special insights, both as a Torah scholar and as a *tzaddik*' a spiritual leader—of our generation. In *The Rebbe's Advice*, you will read first-hand how Torah has the answers for all of life's issues. A Rebbe not only gives advice based on Torah and its writings, but more specifically based on your unique identity and your soul's destiny. The Rebbe's advice goes far beyond the legalistic, Talmudic, and chasidic; it reflects deep-seated holy insights within him, which manifest as practical recommendations for the seeker.

A rabbi can tell you what Jewish law would advise; a counselor could inform you about the latest ways in improving your character. However, neither can tell you that the advice that is being given is what your soul truly needs. Sometimes we seem to have everything, and yet we are unhappy. Why? Because we are not connecting to the core essence that links us to G-d vis-a-vis Torah. Instead of relying only on general guidelines, the Rebbe directs us in a clear and specific path, and all we have to do is follow it and absorb its meaning. This causes genuine happiness.

Much of the advice in the book is printed in the Rebbe's 23 volumes of his letters, known as *Igros Kodesh*, or in other publications that contain letters, memos, and private audience dialogues written or spoken by the Rebbe. In addition, many people have had the merit to have private audiences with the Rebbe. Some of them have shared the advice they received, because it can be used and applied by others. The advice chosen in this book is that which seems to be the most universal. Any advice which has a private tone to it was not incorporated in the book. Interestingly, the Rebbe himself instructed that many of his responses may and should be shared by others, even though initially they were said or written to individuals.

It must be stated clearly and unequivocally that the Rebbe's advice should be compared to the statement made in *Ethics of the Fathers*: "Learn it, learn it, because everything is in it"—referring to the Torah. In truth, everything is in

Torah, but it is our shortsightedness that obscures the advice. A *tzaddik* like the Rebbe is an individual who has 'clear vision' and does see the answer to our personal questions. If I may say it, the Rebbe is a 'walking Torah'!

Because of this, the Rebbe's advice to an individual is relevant to all others as well. Again, think of Torah. Torah speaks many times in general terms, yet every word is relevant as practical guidance to each person. The instruction is given in general terms and each person must find a way of making it fit his personal circumstances. In the same vein, the advice a *tzaddik* gives, even if it was given to a certain person in a unique context, is relevant to all others who find themselves struggling with the same issue. As a practical matter, however, since our circumstances are always different, one must use the guidance as general instruction. The exact application at any given time must be discussed with a competent rabbi, counselor of Torah, and most preferably a Lubavitcher *chasid* (see Epilogue).

There may be times when reading a letter or hearing it from a friend does not satisfy one's dilemma. Therefore one should exercise the rule mentioned in *Ethics of Our Fathers*: "One who does not question does not know how to learn." If you feel I have left out an important area in seeking the Rebbe's advice, feel free to contact me. Also, if you have a letter or any other relevant correspondence from the Rebbe in which advice is given that is not incorporated in this book, please contact me.

May we merit to be re-united with our holy Rebbe, culminating with Moshiach's arrival now, Amen!

Rabbi Chaim Dalfin. received his rabbinical ordination from the Central Yeshiva Tomchei Temimim Lubavitch in Brooklyn, New York. He received his Ph.D. in Psychology from Pacific Western University in California. Rabbi Dalfin is professor emeritus of Jewish Mysticism at the West Coast Talmudic Seminary. He is the author of *Your Better Self* (1994), a book on the chasidic approach to self-improvement; *Demystifying the Mystical* (1995), a primer to ease the beginner into the esoteric world of mysticism and chasidism; *Conversations with the Rebbe* (1996), interviews with 14 Jewish figures about Rabbi Schneerson; *To Be Chasidic* (1996), a contemporary guide into chasidism exploring its history, founding principles, ideology, and practices; and *The Rebbe's Advice* (1997), practical advice on social, health & business issues. He is the recording artist of the Chasidic Melodies Series- Learn, Understand, and Sing - 4 volumes. Rabbi Dalfin lives with his wife and five children in Brooklyn, New York.

Rabbi Dalfin invites your comments or questions.
1721 45th Street Brooklyn, NY 11204
(718) 854-4139 Fax (718) 438-7628
Email: dalfin@worldnet.att.net
www. jewishinfo.org

To All Readers

The accuracy of the translation of the Rebbe's answers which are contained in this book are the sole responsibility of the author and were not edited or authorized by the Rebbe.

If one wants to use any of this advice, one must consult with a qualified Rabbi.

The Rebbe's general advice was when there is a question about health, one should consult a doctor who is a friend, and also to consult with specialists in that field. About financial problems, one should consult friends for advice, and about spiritual and personal concerns one should consult a Rav, as it says in Ethics of Our Fathers "Make for yourself a Rav."

This book is not a substitute for getting medical help.

Mendelsohn Press

THE REBBE'S ADVICE

1
CLOTHING AND APPEARANCE

Each day new garment

Unfortunately, the *galus* is so great that people are constantly indulging in such materialism as clothing. Every day one feels he needs to wear a new garment different than the day before. If he does not have this change daily, his *nefesh habahamis* (animal drive) feels lacking!

Sichos Kodesh, 5722, p. 109

Wearing the same *sirtug* (chasidic frock) for 120 years

In 1968 the Rebbe spoke about launching an offensive war in matters of Jewishness. There were complaints from other religious groups that such a practice was not done by our ancestors. Why the innovation? To this the Rebbe responded:

Your grandfather had a room of 4 amos (cubits), he ate meat only on Shabbos, and he wore his wedding sirtug until 120. When the bride sewed a dress for her wedding, it remained hanging in her closet until her daughter's and granddaughter's wedding.

You complainers, you are dressed with 18 different garments, all at the same time! In all your matters things have changed and you do not conduct yourself as your grandfathers, yet in regard to helping another Jew, you want to be like your grandfathers and remain home, not going out to battle the spiritual war of assimilation! First be like your grandparents in matters of materiality, and then worry about emulating them by staying inside.

Sefer HaShlichus, p. 68

Clean clothing

The previous Rebbe instructed the students of *Tomchei Temimim* to dress properly, cleanly, neatly, and that their speech should be clear and organized.

Askila b'Derech Tomim, p. 184

Polishing the shoes

Rabbi Chodokov cautioned the students who would go on *Merkos Shlichus* (visiting Jews in communities worldwide) to make sure they polish their shoes so that they cause a *kiddush Hashem*. When a person sees that your shoes are not polished and dirty, this makes a bad impression of what *chasidus*, Lubavitch, and the Rebbe stand for.

Oral communication to author

Right over left

On Friday, the 14th of Menachem Av, 1981, after the Rebbe arrived at 770, he distributed coins to the children standing outside to put into tzedaka. One boy had a shirt that had a picture of some superstar on it. The Rebbe asked him if he belongs to Tzivos Hashem. He said yes. The Rebbe asked him why he is wearing such a shirt.

One afternoon about a month later, after the conclusion of mincha, the Rebbe stared very intently at a boy standing close by. The Rebbe approached his grandfather, pointing out that on the boy's shirt appeared to be something that looked like a cross and that it should be corrected, and that this is particularly this is important with children. At ma'ariv time, the boy had changed into a Tzivos Hashem shirt. The next day the Rebbe acknowledged the correction.

Yuman Hakhel, 5741, pp. 164 & 174

Single-breasted suit

Many times the Rebbe emphasized the vital importance of wearing one's clothing in a manner that the right side of a suit is over the left, not visa versa. This is basically because right represents kindness and goodness, whereas left represents judgement and harshness. A Jew should practice the right (chesed) over the left (gevura), not the opposite.

A person was wearing a single-breasted suit, with the left side of the jacket buttoned over the right side.

The Rebbe noticed it and told him to tell his mother to sew a button on the inside of the right side, enabling him to button the right side over the left side.

Hiskashrus, Volume 40, p. 12

Increasing parnasa

Someone came to the Rebbe to receive a brocha for his parnasa, since it was not good. The Rebbe told him to ask a tailor to change his button of his jacket so that the right side will be over the left. The Rebbe noticed it was left over right. The Rebbe told him that by doing this his parnasa would increase.

Hiskashrus, Volume 40, p. 12

Beard and peyos

Our sages teach that we were liberated in the merit of not changing our names and clothing while our ancestors were in Egypt. The Previous Rebbe, in *Likutei Dibburim* (Volume 3, p. 406a) says this includes the wearing of a beard and side locks (*peyos*). However, this is in addition to the literal meaning that the outside appearance of a Jew"s clothing should be Jewish, not *goyish*.

Igros Kodesh, Volume 20, p. 312

Color of Shabbos clothing

A bar-mitzvah boy asked the Rebbe about wearing colored clothing on *Shabbos* and *Yom Tov*. The Rebbe responded:

It is well known that some people wear white on

Chapter 1 / Clothing and Appearance

Shabbos, some wear the opposite (black), and some wear colored.

We, (Lubavitcher *chasidim*) follow the practice of the Rebbe our leader, my saintly father-in-law.

Hiskashrus, Volume 31, p. 10

The previous Rebbe wore a white shirt and a black *sirtug* on Shabbos.

Silk garment on Shabbos and Yom Tov

The Rebbe told Rabbi Zev Greenglass that it is about time that all young married men wear *zidene zubetzes* (silk coats) on *Shabbos* and *Yom Tov*. This idea is mentioned in a *ma'amor* of the Rebbe Rashab.

Toras Menachem, Volume 1, p. 53

Girls dressing up as boys

In regard to play performances that are put on in school, be careful not to violate the prohibition of "a man's wear should not be worn by a woman."

Igros Kodesh, Volume 10, p. 238

This seems to imply that a child dressing up in the clothing of the opposite gender is inappropriate.

Men wearing rings

In your letter you write that, based on your reading in *seforim*, you have made yourself a silver ring and engraved holy names of *Hashem* on it. You ask if you should wear it on your hand as a remedy.

As far as I know, in your community, only women wear rings. Therefore, for a man to wear a ring would possibly be in violation of "a man is not allowed to wear women's clothing." This is in addition to the difficulty of engraving holy names of Hashem into a ring and wearing in places which are not holy, such as dirty and filthy public streets.

I suggest you do not wear the ring. Put it away in the room you sleep in.

Igros Kodesh, Volume 7, p. 248

Black hat

Someone who recently became religious asked the Rebbe if he should put on a long coat and a black hat, even though his family opposed this. The Rebbe responded:

Since you yourself have doubts as to whether or not you should do this, it is better to refrain and reevaluate at a later date. If one makes these significant changes, it has to come from a place of clarity and sureness. Otherwise, it is possible that later on, when people scoff and laugh at you because of your strange dress, you will feel the pressure and change back into your current dress.

Igros Kodesh, Volume 12, p. 330

Schochet wearing long coat

A *schochet* asked the Rebbe whether he should put on a long coat, since in the place where he slaughters, the other *schochtim* wear long coats. The Rebbe told him not to stand out, particularly because it will be seen as a leniency in observance of Torah and *mitzvos*, and to follow the dress code is by wearing a long coat.

Igros Kodesh, Volume 10, p. 93

The seemingly contradictory advice between the last two letters can be resolved. In the first case, it was a person who recently found his roots, and his general changes were enough for his family to deal with. Adding drastic external changes would really disturb his family who could put lots of pressure on him and cause him to revert to his old ways. In the second case, the person was a long-time schochet for whom there were no concerns of being insulted for his new dress code; on the contrary, the others would look up to him because of it.

Modern clothing for shidduch purposes

You write that you have been proposed a *shidduch* with a women who desires that you exchange your clothing for more modern ones.

It is understood that such a demand is not acceptable, since it reflects the level of the women and/or her family. If these are the types of conditions they want at this juncture, one already knows their future demands, which will diminish your level of commitment.

Hiskashrus, Volume 10, p. 13

Protection from bad friends

Your husband is right in demanding that your son wear the same style clothing as he has been wearing until now. New designs, clothing that is more fashionable, will give him more access to bad company. By wearing the regular conventional style, this in and of itself will reduce the possibility of his meeting undesirable friends.

Igros Kodesh, Volume 12, p. 335

Wearing suit for rabbinic audition

A Rabbi received an offer in a shul where the congregants were not wearing long coats on Shabbos, as was his practice. He asked the Rebbe whether he should wear a suit instead, just for that Shabbos. The Rebbe responded:

I do not see that wearing a kapote can weaken your position there. On the contrary, it is possible that they will wonder why is a Rabbi, who has a beard, is dressing in a suit on Shabbos and on Yom Tov during his speech before Yizkor.

Igros Kodesh, Volume 5, p. 291

Women's modest dress

The Rebbe explained a Gemora at the end of tractate Sotah which states that the youth will embarrass the elders, a daughter will rise against her mother, and a daughter-in-law against her mother-in-law in the following way:

The mother wears a sheitel that exposes some hair because some non-Jew in Paris decided that one's hair should show. Along comes the daughter and announces, "I am not embarrassed and I will wear a sheitel that covers my entire hair!" She walks in the streets this way and is not fazed by what the goy in Paris says.

The daughter continues to say, "The fact that some

goy in Paris decided that one should wear a short skirt does not change my practice. I listen to Moshe Rabbeinu, l'havdil, who taught that a woman's modesty is royalty." This behavior will bring true Jewish nachas from one's children.

Sichos Kodesh, 5728, Volume 1, p. 229

Tznius and Moshiach

The Rebbe said that in today's day and age (1991), especially in the last year, there has been an increase in *tznius* in the type of clothing available to women. This clothing does not cause a husband or brother to have inappropriate thoughts; on the contrary, the clothes emphasizes that *tznius* is royalty.

This opportunity itself brings closer the redemption.

Hisva'adiyus, 5751, Volume 1, pp. 142-143

Dresses and shorts

The Rebbe said that it is easier to be more *tzniusdik*, since the president of the United States has ordered that all female government employees must wear dresses at work. *Tznius* clothing includes men as well, particularly in the summer when some men tend to be lenient.

I saw a picture of a "*Spitz* (considers himself great chasid) Chabad," *chasid* in the country wearing shorts!

Farbrengen, Parshas Teruma, 5741

Shliach needs two pairs of shoes and kapotes

In yechidus, the Rebbe told Rabbi Boruch Shlomo Cunin of Los Angeles that a *shliach* must have two pairs of shoes and *kapotes*, so that when one is dirty there will be another to wear.

Oral communication to author

2

TORAH CLASSES, KOLLEL

Chapter 41 in *Tanya segula* for problems

Someone wrote the Rebbe about a problem he was having. The Rebbe responded with surprise that he did not know by heart the beginning of chapter 41 in *Tanya* and had not internalized it in his heart. The idea of that section in *Tanya* is that Hashem stands over a person and sees everything he is doing, speaking, and thinking.

This section of *Tanya* should also be written on paper and be in your pocket at all times. Additionally, it should written in your heart and be with you wherever and whenever.

Nelcha b'Urchosav, p. 227

Must get paid

To study in Kollel, (post graduate yeshiva) without being paid is not a good idea.

Sefer Hechel Menachem, Volume 3, p. 177

Kabbalah lectures

Someone sent the Rebbe an article she wrote on the number three from a kabbalistic view. She intended to use it as a platform for a lecture she was going to give, where both Jews and non-Jews would attend.

The Rebbe made several general comments.

In every thing a person does, the hope is that there be a continuation and positive result. Those people who will attend the talk will not walk away knowing how to learn Kabbalah. More so, they will not be moved to study it. Most importantly, it is not Kabbalah that these people are missing but rather, for most participants, a basic knowledge in the fundamentals of the Torah and *mitzvos*. The non-Jewish participants are not aware of their *mitzvos*, the Seven Noachide Laws.

If you are going to elaborate on the number three, I suggest basic ideas associated with "three" e.g., Torah, *avoda*, and *gemilas chasadim*, with an explanation of their details. Or you could explain the concepts of Kohen, Levi, and Israel, how each one of these three serves Hashem in his particular way, and how every person possesses an element of these three. If you will add these suggestions to your planned talk, emphasize the points so that they are not "swallowed" by the esoteric explanations.

Nelcha b'Urchosav, p. 240

Chapter 2 / Torah Classes, Kollel

Seemingly, the Rebbe is not dismissing classes in Kabbalah as a way to draw people. He is suggesting that since the most important thing in any matter is its continuation and result, one should bring Kabbalah down to earth by teaching the participants the practical application of the esoteric and the exoteric. He suggests using very tangible and practical ideas.

Enthusiasm for Kollel

If one has a doubt whether or not to go to *Kollel*, it is not worthwhile to attend, because *Kollel* participation requires excitement and enthusiasm. If one is doubtful, it shows that one is not excited and probably apathetic to the entire idea.

Sefer Hechel Menachem, Volume 3, p. 178

Returning to Kollel after long interval

Most people do not have the peace of mind needed to learn in Kollel after being involved in some other work, including communal activity. Therefore, I do not recommend that you go back to *Kollel*.

Sefer Hechel Menachem, Volume 3, p. 179

Kollel is made for mature, responsible adults

It is established that a *Kollel* participant must be an adult who is very mature, has set opinions and values, and yearns to learn Torah; whoever considers himself such a person does not need someone to stand over him, constantly reminding him of what he should be doing, namely, learning Torah.

Nelcha b'Urchosav, p. 215

Can a Jew who converted to Christianity join a Torah-study group?

A Jew in Russia wrote that, in a certain city in Russia, there are Jews who converted to Christianity, but some of them now feel an urge towards Judaism and would like to join a Torah-study group. What should be the attitude towards them?

In general, each individual has to be considered as a separate case, and the criterion for admission to the study group should be an assessment of the expected result: Is the individual likely to return to Judaism by attending the Torah study, or will it have the opposite effect?

In making such an assessment, two kinds of individuals should be borne in mind. There may be one who has become a missionary. In this case, he should not be judged in "the scale of merit." Moreover, it is in the nature of such a convert to seek "justification" for his conversion at every opportunity. Hence, he will not stop at deliberately distorting and misrepresenting the truth.

A further factor is this: The Torah classes are attended by Jews, not all of whom are 100% firmly entrenched in Judaism; some of them are rather weak and have doubts. Consequently, if these were to meet with the said element in an atmosphere of Torah learning and

Chapter 2 / Torah Classes, Kollel

discussion, the association may be very harmful to them in view of the weakness of their own convictions.

On the other hand, there is a second type of convert, namely, those who converted not because they have been brainwashed, but for some foolish external reasons, and more particularly those who come under the category of *"Tinokos shenishbu."* In this case, the prospect of helping them return to Judaism is, of course, more promising.

The above are general guidelines, and each individual case should be considered on its own merits, as mentioned.

In addition, there are other general points to be considered:

In view of the holocaust which was largely an outgrowth of centuries-long animosity and persecution systematically perpetrated against Jews, if there is a Jew who, despite living in such close proximity in time and place to this atrocity, yet finds it proper in his mind and heart to become a part of, and be identified with, the creed and its proponents who claimed so many innocent Jewish victims, men, women, and children, all in the name of christianity then perhaps it may be possible to bring him back to his senses in other ways, but hardly by means of Torah lessons.

At the same time, considering those among the study circle members who are so-called border-line cases, whose Jewish identity is still weak and who have to be strengthened in their commitment to Torah, it is easy to see how harmful it would be for them to come into close association with that element, all the more so since it would be difficult to limit such association to the periods of Torah study and preclude them from meeting afterwards in other situation.

Letter, *Cheshvan*, 5739

Mixed Torah classes

A person living in Russia during the trying times of the late 1970s asked the Rebbe whether a group of young women who want to learn Torah could be admitted to men's study classes, or whether separate classes should be formed. In the latter case, would it be proper to have male instructors?

The Rebbe answered:

In view of the extraordinary circumstances and difficulties in that country (Russia), I would be inclined to take a more lenient view to admit women into the men's classes. However, in order to emphasize the exception due to the extenuating circumstances, and also in order to be mindful of the *Din*, two provisions should be made:

One, you must teach in a co-ed class such subjects as are incumbent also on women, such as laws obligatory for women (*kashrus*, laws of *Shabbos* and *Yom Tov*, etc.), and, of course, also the basics of our faith, love and fear of G-d, prayer, and the like subjects that are dealt with in *chasidus*.

Second, separate seating should be arranged for the men and women. This would preclude also other personal associations, such as mixed dancing, etc. And although we are speaking of persons who, by reason of background, are not otherwise averse to mixed dancing and socializing, it is obvious that this should not be permitted in these groups, and no "*hetter*" should be given for such practices, explicit or implied.

I must emphasize again that the "*hetter*" mentioned above in regard to co-ed study is based on the special extenuating circumstances prevailing in that particular country, there being no other way to save them from assimilation and intermarriage. It should in no way serve as a precedent for other countries where those circumstances do not prevail, nor continue even in that same country when the situation improves sufficiently not to have recourse to that "*hetter*."

Letter in archives, 5739

> From the Rebbe's words, the situation in Russia has today changed quite drastically for the good. Therefore, one must consult a Rav whether it would still be considered "extenuating circumstances" still exist to permit mixed classes. The same would be true in other societies; is the assimilation rate considered "extenuating circumstances," thus warranting mixed classes in the United States, for example? One must consult a Rav for a specific ruling in each particular case. Regardless of the rulings that rabbis will give, from the Rebbe's letter it is clear that it is considered a "leniency" and we need to do whatever is possible to mitigate it.

Learning in a yeshiva

To say "thank you" or, in the terminology of our holy sages, to bring a thanksgiving offering, in practice means to dedicate the first year of one's arrival in Eretz Yisrael to learning Torah and doing *mitzvos* in a yeshiva environment.

Igros Kodesh, Volume 19, p. 182

Preventing girl from living with mother who lives with non-Jew

In response to your question as to what to do about a mother who wants her daughter, who has been learning in *Beis Rivka* (girls' school) for quite a while, to leave the school and return home. The mother is currently living with a non-Jew.

The importance is self-understood of making the greatest effort to try to stop this. Surely you will find a lawyer who can advise you on the legalities. It might be worthwhile, if legally it is acceptable, to send the girl to learn in a yeshiva in Israel.

Sefer Hechel Menachem, Volume 3, p. 156

Studying Kabbalah

You write that you heard I told someone to get involved in the learning of Kabbalah. Although in our day and age forgetfulness is frequent, I am not at all accustomed to give such instruction. What I do advise is to learn *chasidus*, which has been revealed in our generation through the teachings of the Baal Shem Tov and the Alter Rebbe.

Igros Kodesh, Volume 20, p. 119

Learning sichos in bed

Students in one of the Lubavitcher yeshivas would nightly fall asleep reading the previous Rebbe's *sichos*. The question was asked whether this is appropriate or

Chapter 2 / Torah Classes, Kollel

whether the administration should suggest that the students stop doing this because it is not respectful.

The Rebbe responded that they should continue doing so.

Nelcha b'Urchosav, p. 212

3

CHINUCH, EDUCATION

Do not forget your days in Tomchei Temimim

Someone said that he once learned in *Yeshivas Tomchei Temimim*. The Rebbe told him not to forget what he learned there; they invested much into him, and he should use it in a positive way.

Zoreah Tzedakos, p. 136

Staying Home

This letter was written as a response to a father's desire to have his children stay at home rather than attend a school in which the standard of Jewish studies was not up to par in the chasidic atmosphere he wanted for his children.

It is understood that it is better to educate children

in an environment where there are other (appropriate) children rather than them being by themselves at home.
Sefer Hechel Menachem, Volume 3, p. 192

> One should consult a Rov before implementing this advice, since the Rebbe himself writes "appropriate;" which kind of a school, with what kind of children, is considered in this category? Only after consultation with a Rav, mashpia, etc., can this be decided properly.

Giving Prizes

Someone told the Rebbe that his daughter does not want to say *brochos*; what can he do to get her to make the *brochos* on her own?

The Rebbe answered:

As the Rambam states, give her a prize.
Sefer Hechel Menachem, Volume 3, pp. 192-193

Hospital a place for outreach

You have the opportunity to reach out to those patients who find themselves with you in the hospital. By helping them increase their Jewishness, which is their spiritual health, Hashem reciprocates by giving good physical health to the one who was diligent in reaching out to others.
Sefer Hechel Menachem, Volume 3, p. 108

Leaving yeshiva to learn a trade

I have already told your mother that there is no reason for alarm merely because your brother wants to pursue a trade. For your brother to be part of the world of

Chapter 3 / Chinuch, Education

Zevulun, i.e., to make a livelihood and financially support the people who learn Torah and their institutions, and additionally to set times for himself to study *nigla* and *chasidus*, is a good thing.

A person does not know what part of the world he needs to refine. Since your brother has already tried learning in yeshiva and has worked diligently to make a success of it, but has not found it to work, it is proper for him to try another approach towards fulfilling his mission in life.

Maybe the best way for him to accomplish his desire is to study in a yeshiva which offers learning a trade as well, or perhaps in conjunction with studying in yeshiva for several hours daily, he should learn a trade. Naturally, the yeshiva should be a religious one.

Igros Kodesh, Volume 21, p. 443

> It must be stated clearly that before one jumps to the conclusion that he is not a candidate to continue learning in a yeshiva, he must consult his parents, mashpia, and Rav.

Benefit of School Tests

The lesson one can take from having to take tests in school is that each person must test himself in matters of holiness, Torah and *mitzvos*. These holy tests are not just once a week or once a month, but daily, as the Alter Rebbe says in *Tanya*, chapter 41: "And, behold, Hashem stands over him, and the whole world is full with His Glory, and he tests him, and searches his reins and heart to see if he is serving Him as is fitting."

Sefer Hechel Menachem, Volume 3, p. 168

Getting Children to Listen

A woman told the Rebbe that her son is causing her great pain by not listening to her advice about a certain issue.

The Rebbe told her that she should be aware that in today's day and age, a parent can influence a son or daughter when the advice comes from a good friend. If the same words come from a parent, it has very little results. Many times, when parents advise their grown children, the son or daughter considers it as though he is being spoken to as a little child.

Zoreah Tzedakos, p. 140

Once a Tomim, always a Tomim

The Rebbe told someone who said he once learned in the Lubavitcher yeshiva, *Tomchei Temimim*, "Once you have learned in *Tomchei Temimim*, you are a *Tomim* the rest of your life. You have no choice!"

Zoreah Tzedakos, p. 136

Students who ask questions but don't want answers

With regard to your question whether you should always reply to the queries of the boys in the class, who, it seems to you, are not as much interested in the replies as in stating their views, etc., it is particularly advisable to avoid leaving the impression with them that their questions are unanswerable. For, inasmuch as their questions are connected with matters of Torah and *mitzvos*, the fact that they would remain unanswered might in some way weaken their observance.

On the other hand, experience shows that it is no good to engage in long (and empty) discussions, which are likely to be more wasteful than useful. Therefore, you should try to find the middle road between these two extremes, and, inasmuch as you know the boys for a relatively considerable length of time, you will surely find the proper balance as to how far to engage in discussions.

Teshura Nagel, *Lag B'Omer*, 5757, p. 75

Thanksgiving offering increasing Torah and mitzvos

It is brought down in many *seforim* that, when one experiences a miracle, one should meditate on the greatness of Hashem Who performs miracles, and one should bring a thanksgiving sacrifice by adding to his study of Torah and performance of *mitzvos*.

Igros Kodesh, Volume 13, p. 464

Chabad korbon Todah

It is superfluous to mention that the thanksgiving offering by *Anash* (Lubavitcher followers) and *chasidim* is an increase in one's learning of *chasidus* and disseminating the wellsprings of *chasidus* to others as yet unfamiliar with its teachings.

Igros Kodesh, Volume 13, p. 432

Tehillim blesses the month

The saying of the entire book of *Tehillim* before davening on *Shabbos Mevorchim* (the *Shabbos* that precedes the new month) is a preparation and gives power to bless the upcoming new month, which is blessed during davening.

Sichos Kodesh, 5715, p. 114

Authentic commentary

The few short lines before each chapter in *Tehillim*, although we do not know who wrote them, are nonetheless authentic. They give us a brief insight into the chapter. The fact that this commentary has been published in the printed *Tehillim* proves its validity.

Hisva'adiyus, 5747, Volume 1, p. 81

Understanding what you are reading

The reason there has not been a formal study of *Tehillim* in yeshivas and *chadarim*, similar to the study of *Gemora* and *Chumash*, is that the teachers have believed it is more important to have a *Rosh yeshiva* and *melamed* spend their time teaching the student the intricacies of *Gemora*, enabling them to learn on their own, than to teach *Tehillim*. *Tehillim*, they felt, the students can pick up on their own.

The sad fact is that they do not know the meaning of the words of *Tehillim*!

Hisva'adiyus, 5742, Volume 2, p. 358

Chapter 3 / Chinuch, Education

It must be stated that regardless of the importance of knowing the translation of the words of Tehillim, a person should say Tehillim on a regular basis although they might not know the meaning. The words themselves are sweet.

4
HEALTH AND MEDICINE

Overweight

Someone wrote the Rebbe that he is overweight and is very worried about it, and that it is very difficult for him to refrain from overeating.

The Rebbe said that, first of all, the doctors are exaggerating their evaluation of the damage that can be caused by the extra weight. Secondly, he should stop thinking about this issue on a regular basis. Its removal from his mind will in itself diminish the need to overeat and will make him feel calmer, which will help him metabolize the fat intake.

Most importantly, he should serve Hashem with joy.

Nelcha b'Urchosav, p. 219

Cure for heart attacks

Someone told the Rebbe he had had two heart attacks, and asked for a brocha to feel better.

The Rebbe said that the fulfillment of "loving Hashem with all your heart" requires a healthy heart;

therefore he should do what he is supposed to, and Hashem will do His part.

Zoreah Tzedakos, p. 118

Give a kiddush on Simchas Torah

A person told the Rebbe that a year and a half earlier he had received a *brocha* for a difficult operation which he needed and now, after the operation, he is asking that he feel better.

The Rebbe responded by asking him if he danced with the Torah the *Simchas Torah* following his operation. The person said he made a *seudas mitzvah* to thank Hashem for getting through the serious operation, but he did not do it on *Simchas Torah*.

The Rebbe told him that he needed to dance, not just for himself and his recovery, but for the Torah as well. Therefore, he should make it up the following *Simchas Torah*. Until then he would be blessed with a healing of the body, and surely with a healthy soul, through the learning of Torah and performance of *mitzvos*.

Zoreah Tzedakos, p. 117

Autistic children

The Rebbe told someone who mentioned that his daughter is autistic:

Hashem should bless you to have much Jewish pride from her. There is a professor who is an expert in this field somewhere in the United States, I think in Cleveland. It would be worthwhile for you to contact him.

Zoreah Tzedakos, p. 120

Chapter 4 / Health and Medicine

Remedy for relaxation

This was written to someone whose father was in the hospital and was feeling very unrelaxed. The son asked the Rebbe for advice as to help his father relax.

Bring him a *Tanya* and every so often read it to him. Also, put a checked *mezuzah*, double-wrapped in an envelope, in his room.

Sefer Hechel Menachem, Volume 3, p. 144

Bitter and sweet pills

Based on the Rambam's words, every soul has its health and illness, just as does the body. The human body, when ill, can be cured in two ways:

1. By taking bitter tasting pills, or
2. Sweet tasting pills.

The difference is self-understood, particularly when the pills are needed several times daily. These two types apply to the soul as well. The bitter type of cure are the teachings known as *mussar* (moral ethical teachings), emphasizing the no-good character aspects of one's personality. The sweet pill would be the teachings of *chasidus*, which emphasize the elevated special stature of the soul.

I recommend that you organize a set time to learn *chasidus*, which will bring a spiritual cure to your soul.

Igros Kodesh, Volume 17, p. 55

Stay away from hypnosis

I would like to make a further point, though not

entirely in my domain, namely, in reference to hypnosis as one of the techniques used in psychotherapy, as mentioned in your letter.

I have always been wary of any method that deprives a person of the free exercise of his will, and which puts him in the power of another person, even temporarily except, of course, in a case of *pikuach nefesh* (saving a life). Certainly I would not favor the use of such a method on a wider scale, least of all to encourage psychologists and psychiatrists enrolled in our program to use it.

Letter, *Adar*, 5738

This letter was written to a psychologist who was encouraged by the Rebbe to enroll other professionals to develop a kosher program for Jewish Meditation. This is what the Rebbe means when he writes "our program."

Auspices of Jewish Meditation Institute

The suggestion that an institute employing the said healing techniques might be linked with a strictly orthodox, even Lubavitch, orientation should be examined in light of it being a possible, or even likely, deterrent for many candidates who might hesitate to turn to such an Institute for fear that it may impose upon them religious demands and commitments which they are not yet prepared to accept.

The above is not to say that the idea should be rejected out of hand, since there may be individuals who would not be deterred by it. But I believe that if the project is to attract a wider circle of candidates for therapy, it would have a wider acceptance if it is not overtly tied in with such an orientation, or discipline; at any rate, not in the initial stage.

Needless to say, the emphasis is on the overt orientation of the projected Institute, which should have no religious or other preconditions for anyone seeking its services. But the Institute itself should, of course be run in strict keeping with the Torah, with a kosher, indeed glatt-kosher, kitchen, strict *Shabbos* observance, with *mezuzos* on all doors just as there are glatt-kosher hotels and institutions.

Letter in archives, 5738

Schizophrenia

Putting on *tefillin* is the aid for all those needing a blessing. Every negative has a positive counterpart. So too, with this illness. The person who is schizophrenic sees the situation with his intellect differently than the reality. Therefore, 1) his emotions correspond to his belief that everyone is trying to hurt him, and 2) he has mood swings, from extreme fear to extreme exaltation, neither one based on reality.

Its remedy, and part of the mitzvah of *tefillin*, is to dedicate the heart (emotions) and the mind (intellect) to Hashem of truth, of Whom it says, "I am Hashem, I do not change." This produces consistency between the mind, heart, and reality.

Sefer Hechel Menachem, Volume 3, pp. 41-42

Hospital is a place for healers

Someone asked the Rebbe for a *brocha* that her grandchild, who was in the hospital (known in Hebrew as *beis hacholim*, or "home for the sick," be healed. The Rebbe said the following:

I am accustomed not to call the institution a "house for the sick," but rather by its true name, *beis harofim* (a house for the healers) since in truth it is a home for the doctors, who are Hashem's healers. The person who is ill became ill in his home. Why are they going away from their home to another location? It is because this other location is a place of healing.

Zoreah Tzedakos, p. 118

Cancer "that" illness

A woman asked the Rebbe for a *brocha* for someone who had "that" illness. (This is a reference to cancer, which is unfortunately today's least curable sickness. Therefore, it has been called with the word "that," the known one.)

The Rebbe said, when we say the word "that," it implies something in the far distance. However, the illness should have no association with the person whatsoever.

Zoreah Tzedakos, p. 119

5.
TZEDAKA

Hiskashrus

...In addition to thinking and speaking the Rebbe's Torah and doing the Rebbe's wishes, one needs to involve his mind, heart, willpower, and pleasure. This activity binds a person with all their soul powers to the Rebbe.

However, every person knows that from time to time he lacks the proper *hiskashrus* (bonding) in one specific soul quality. How does one accomplish *hiskashrus* when that is in effect?

The solution is through giving *tzedaka*. The person's money could have been used for his own necessities, but instead he gives it away. This generosity reflects his dedication to Hashem, as explained in *Tanya*, chapter 37.

Specifically, this applies when one gives *tzedaka* in a manner known as *shibuda d'reb Noson*. This refers to Rabbi Noson's statement in the Talmud which says that if Shimon loans money to Levi and Levi does not have the money to pay back, and that Reuven happens to owe

Levi money, Shimon is allowed to get his money from Reuven. This is because Levi's possessions are "mortgaged" to Shimon.

In the same vein, when a person "mortgages" himself to the Rebbe, he dedicates himself to whatever the Rebbe is mortgaged to!

Likutei Sichos, Volume 4, p. 1325

Guards from evil eye

I received your note and the *tzedaka* which is being given to the "private fund"; this fund is completely private in its nature. The people who receive from this fund are those who would not ask for assistance, because it is not according to their honor to do so.

It is known that anything which is covered from the eye is protected from an evil eye.

So too, may the merit of your *tzedaka* stand by you so that Hashem will give you His blessings with a good eye and protect you from an eye that is no good.

Igros Kodesh, Volume 10, p. 280

Curing foot aches: contributing to educational institutions

A Jew's physicality and spirituality go together. The sages explain the verse, "*yikum asher bragleihem*" (Deuteronomy 11:6), as a reference to one's money.

(Literally the verse refers to Doson and Aviram, who were swallowed alive into the earth because they joined Korach in rebelling against Moshe and Aron. The

Torah says that they went with their houses, tents, and feet which sustain the person in the sense that, without the feet, one would not be able to stand upright. Likewise, this applies to a person's money, which sustains the person).

It is appropriate for you to increase your *tzedaka*, particularly to educational institutions which are involved with the education of Jewish children. Children are the future of our people and consequently are indeed the ones who sustain the Jewish nation.

Igros Kodesh, Volume 19, p. 103

Give tzedaka before visiting the doctor

The reason we are instructed to give *tzedaka* before davening is that the person requests of Hashem to fulfill his personal needs; by fulfilling another person's needs, Hashem reciprocates and answers the person's call.

Giving *tzedaka* before visiting a doctor is necessary, since going to a doctor is associated with a negative predicament in one's health; therefore the need to give *tzedaka* is even greater to bring Hashem's blessing into your life.

Hisva'adiyus, 5747, Volume 1, p. 382

Reducing real estate problems

You inform me that a year ago you bought a home in another neighborhood and are constantly having problems. (Seemingly it was an investment and the owner was having problems associated with the property).

Many times this happens because one is not as careful as he should be in fulfilling the mitzvah of tithing from the profits of the real estate investment, the home. Even if in your case you have not tithed until now, you should tithe now. Additionally, you should give to *tzedaka* the amount of money you were supposed to tithe but did not.

Igros Kodesh, Volume 16, p. 101

Business venture going sour

I hear that some of your business branches are not going the way you hoped. Surely you need to look at this as a test given to you by Hashem. Although Hashem knows that a Jew's heart is always open and willing to study Torah and perform *mitzvos*, yet in order to prove it to the heavenly court and the angels, who do not believe it until proven, Hashem says "look, see for yourself." Although the evil inclination tries to convince the Jew to decrease his amount of giving *tzedaka*, giving the excuse that business is not the way it was in the past. Regardless, Jews are intelligent and understand that this a test, and when they will succeed in their challenge by revealing the true purpose of the test, not only will the business be successful as before, but more so, it will be much better.

The reason it will produce much more than before is understood from an analogy. A father loves when his son understands all that he does. The greater the son displays his wisdom the more the father gives him presents. So also, business people say that the longer they are in business the better they understand its workings.

Therefore, since you have been in business a long time, you should understand Hashem's intent in the given situation, just as if it were a good investment in a hotel, when you would not invest a limited amount, but rather you would invest as much as possible. So too in regard to *tzedaka*: You need increase it, knowing that Hashem will fulfill His part as promised in the Torah that by tithing one becomes wealthy and you, Hashem's partner, will make much more than ever before.

Igros Kodesh, Volume 7, p. 337

Remedy for bitochan

At night, read the *Shema*, and before that give several coins to *tzedaka*. This will intensify your trust in Hashem.

Igros Kodesh, Volume 6, p. 274

Having male children

In response to your request that a blessing be given for your wife to have healthy male children, it is proper to increase your *ahavas Yisrael*, *ha'Torah*, and Hashem. As explained in *chasidus* and kabbalah, the spiritual aspect of love is a remedy to have male offspring. These three types of spiritual love are accessed through contemplating on Hashem's greatness. This causes long good life to the male children, who are born because of the spiritual male quality that was motivated.

Additionally, *bli neder* (without taking a vow), until after your wife gives birth to a boy, you should give some *tzedaka* each day before davening, and it would be a good idea if the particular charity fund is to feed poor students. When you will have the baby boy, give him a name after my saintly father-in-law, which is Yosef Yitzchak.

Igros Kodesh, Volume 7, p. 51

Bikur cholim fund

I received your letter in which you write about feeling depressed about your overall health situation.

Surely you have a set time for learning *nigla* and *chasidus* and you recite the daily portion of *Tehillim* as divided by the month, after *shachris* daily. Preferably, on Monday and Thursday before davening, you should give *tzedaka* to a *bikur cholim* (visiting the sick) charity.

Igros Kodesh, Volume 8, p. 111

Tithing from future revenues

You inform me that one of your business deals has recently gone into bankruptcy. There is no need to fall into depression, G-d forbid. People in our generations that have witnessed Hashem's open miracles, such as being saved from the Holocaust, can rely on Hashem to change any negative situation to the good.

A person must make a vessel for Hashem's blessing. I urge you to get involved in a business in which you have expertise and in which you can use your talents, and to do this with trust and faith.

Since your work is only a vessel for the blessing, one can therefore understand the importance of increasing your study of Torah and your fulfillment of *mitzvos*. This includes your resolution to tithe a little more than the ten percent required by Jewish law, and it would be best if you could give some right away, even before you actually start making money. This little amount, which is given based on the future revenues, will serve as proof in your trust in Hashem.

Igros Kodesh, Volume 16, p. 28

Diminishing Tzedaka because of decrease in income

You write that you have accustomed yourself over the last 37 years to tithe, but since in the future your income will be reduced and it will be impossible for you to continue giving the same amount you gave in the past, you ask me how to do this, and whether you need to do the ritual of dissolving a vow.

It is a great wonder that you allow yourself into this entire discussion, since you know quite well that the best solution is for you to continue your good old practice of tithing the same amount as in the past. All you have to do is demand of Hashem to give you enough money and health to do the same as in the past. We derive this approach from a law in the opposite vein: The Torah law states that if a person has lived the majority of his life without sin, he will not sin the rest of his remaining years. This is because the Torah follows the majority opinion and situation.

In other words, in this situation, since he had tithed for 37 years,

Hashem guarantees he will have the money to continue tithing the rest of his life; all one has to do is demand of Hashem.

Igros Kodesh, Volume 18, p. 383

Tzedaka when business is not successful

You write you moved your tailoring business to a new location, but so far you do not see any financial success.

Probably you are aware of the importance of tithing from the profits. Particularly when things are financially difficult, one needs to increase his *tzedaka* to at least ten percent. This money should be distributed over several times, not all at once. Among the auspicious times to give is before davening *shachris*. Additionally, check your *tefillin* and ask a Rav if the front door to your store needs a *mezuzah*. If it does, then affix a kosher *mezuzah* in accordance with all requirements as prescribed in the code of Jewish law. If not, then at least make sure that you have in your store a *siddur* and *Tehillim*.

May Hashem grant you much parnasa, and you should increase your Torah study in your free time and influence your friends to do the same. The merit of getting others to do the same will be in good standing for you.

Igros Kodesh, Volume 17, p. 100

Give half now

I am responding to your inquiry as what to do about tithing, since you are currently in a dire financial situation.

I suggest you give half now, while taking the other half upon yourself as a debt which you will pay when your financial status improves.

Igros Kodesh, Volume 17, p. 262

Not contributing to questionable organizations

You inform me that you are accustomed to giving *tzedaka* to many institutions and poor people. However, you have your doubts as to the authenticity of all these institutions, and it is your opinion that certain ones are more legitimate than others in matters of *yiras shomayim*, Torah, and *mitzvos*. You conclude that you would like to give to those which you feel are more honest and stop giving to the others.

These type of thoughts always arouses suspicion as to their true source. Is it from the good side, or the opposite? The negative side has a way of coming to the Jew and blocking him from Torah and *mitzvos*. He does this by first clothing himself in a disguise of religiosity, because he knows if he approaches the Jew and says outright to stop doing a mitzvah, the Jew will not listen to him.

In your case, the first approach of the negative side is to suggest that one institution may not be as honest as another, and therefore I will not give them any more money. From there, he proceeds to convince the person not to give so much money to another institution; it is enough that you gave them last year. The result is now that the organization that was honest, in your opinion, is not getting any more money because you gave them last year, while the other organizations are not getting because, in your humble opinion, they are not worthy.

In general we know the warnings of our sages not to be overly scrupulous in making judgments about which institution or person is worthy, authentic, etc.

The way to deal with your concerns is to dedicate a minimum amount that all kosher institutions will receive, without investigating their religiosity, while those that excel in *yiras shomayim* will receive an additional amount.

Igros Kodesh, Volume 19, p. 163

Dedicating seforim

It is my obligation to emphasize the appropriateness of giving part of the money towards the printing the *seforim* of our holy Rebbeim. This is an eternal merit, since each time the *seforim* are learned from, those who made it possible for the *sefer* to be in existence have a part in the person's learning.

If the contributor's first names and mother's names are mentioned on a page in the back of the *sefer*, the one learning in the *sefer* will notice it and is essentially mentioning them.

(Sometimes there those who object to their family name being mentioned in the dedication, because they are fearful of an evil eye. However, in this case only their first names are being mentioned without the family name.)

Likutei Sichos, Volume 24, p. 431

Extra money in a fund

The extra money that was collected for the *Sefer Torah* should be used for other good and worthy causes associated with Torah and *mitzvos*. This is based on the widespread custom that the directors of a *tzedaka* fund have the right to distribute the extra money to other similar *tzedaka* funds (Particularly because the contributor gave the money with that in mind).

Teshuvos u'Beurim, p. 340

This remark was said on the 13th of Shevat, 5740, to the organizers of a fund collecting money for the writing of a Sefer Torah in honor of the Rebbe and Rebbitzin. The organizers asked the Rebbe what to do with the extra money.

Deeding a property to a yeshiva

In response to your question of wanting to donate a property to the local yeshiva, regarding to whom you should deed it, my opinion is to do it the simplest way. Deed it to the yeshiva itself by putting their name on the deed as the new owners. This is only if the yeshiva has a proper set of legal by-laws. If they do not have their own by-laws, I suggest deeding it to the yeshiva in Lod (Israel), since they are the umbrella organization of your local yeshiva.

Consult a lawyer who will make sure everything is legal, making the donation legal. Surely, you are aware of the importance of supporting and developing the local yeshiva in Rishon l'Tzion (Israel), in addition to other Chabad institutions throughout Israel. As the sages teach, a person is obligated to support the local poor people in his own community before supporting the poor people outside of his city.

Sefer Hechel Menachem, Volume 3, p. 126

This was written to Rabbi Yosef Shmotkin, who lived in Rishon l'Tzion, where there was a Chabad yeshiva.

Flood

Regarding the damage you had from a flood, there are well-known words of the Alter Rebbe to Rabbi M. Dribin, whose boat sunk, saying that after a person has great financial damage, which is an expression of G-d's attribute of judgement, the attribute of mercy is awakened, which is greater than ordinary kindness. G-d's merciful power expresses itself in the wealth that the person then receives.

Igros Kodesh, Volume 5, Letter 1403

The Rebbe is advising the person that not only will he make back what he lost because of the flood but more so, he will become wealthy. (See Rebbe's remarks, printed in *Derech Mitzvohsecha*, p. 419, section beginning with comment on the word "Sereifa"). The Rebbe's reference to the attribute of mercy implies this. Chasidus explains that benevolence coming from the attribute of chesed is limited compared to the kindness based on the attribute of rachmanus. (See my book, *Demystifying the Mystical*, chapter 13, Jason Aronson, 1996.)

6

SHIDDUCHIM, BRIDE AND GROOM, PREGNANCY

Two Marriage choices

Check them both out and pursue the one which feels more appropriate.

Sefer Hechel Menachem, Volume 3, p. 170

Consulting parents

It is customary to consult parents about a perspective *shidduch* before one finalizes his or her decision.

Sefer Hechel Menachem, Volume 3, p. 171

Money

In some communities, the practice is to require the bride's family pay money to the groom before finalizing the shidduch, particularly if the groom sits and learns Torah in yeshiva and plans to continue learning in kollel after marriage. The money is meant to enable the newlywed groom to learn without worries. In other circles, the groom's family is required to pay money to get a special bride with exceptional qualities.

As is known, a *shidduch* should not be rejected for financial reasons.

Sefer Hechel Menachem, Volume 3, p. 172

Sooner than later

My opinion is that, in our day and age, whoever makes the wedding closer to the engagement is praiseworthy. It is not advisable to make a long interval between the engagement and the actual wedding. The sooner, the better.

Sefer Hechel Menachem, Volume 3, p. 173

Husband and wife should learn together

It is very worthwhile that husband and wife should set aside time to learn together those parts in Torah as prescribed in the Alter Rebbe's Shulchan Aruch, laws of *Talmud Torah*, end of chapter 1.

Sefer Hechel Menachem, Volume 3, p. 188

Good offer but I have no job

A person was suggested a shidduch, but he did not have a job and was not planning to go to kollel.

The Rebbe told him that since the girl has many virtues, he should pursue the *shidduch*. On the other

Chapter 6 / Shidduchim, Bride & Groom, Pregnancy

hand, the fact that he does not intend to go to *kollel* and is unemployed means he must formulate a plan for the real possibility of finding a job. Although he will not necessarily have a job, attaining the clarity of which direction to follow, and what potential jobs exist in his field, are prerequisites in his pursuit.

Nelcha b'Urchosav, p. 238

Substitution for yechidus

A bride was scheduled to travel back home from her stay at the Rebbe's community, Crown Heights. If she left according to her planned itinerary, she would miss the bride and groom *yechidus*. She asked the Rebbe if she should forfeit the airline ticket in order to go along with her groom into *yechidus klolis*.

The Rebbe responded that she should not forfeit the ticket. As far as *yechidus*, she should study a *ma'amor chasidus* during the exact time when *yechidus* was taking place. By doing this, the Rebbe said it was as though she actually went into *yechidus*.

Memo in author's archives

When to ask for brocha about healthy pregnancy

It has been handed down from the *chasidim* of the Alter Rebbe, who heard it from his holy mouth in the name of the Baal Shem Tov and Mizritcher Magid, to the members of the Chabad community, that one should not mention that they are pregnant and request a blessing for a healthy child until the end of the third month and the beginning of the fourth month of the pregnancy.

Igros Kodesh Admur Ma'aryatz, Volume 9, p. 451

Going to the mikva during the ninth month of pregnancy

You ask whether your wife should follow her family's custom of immersing herself in the *mikva* after she enters her ninth month. I have not heard from Chabad *chasidim* about such a custom, but since your wife's family does have this custom, therefore, with a doctor's approval that it is not dangerous, do not prevent her from using the *mikva*.

Igros Kodesh, Volume 18, p. 51

Parents may know about pregnancy before five months

The suggesting not to tell people about being pregnant before the fifth month is "not to publicize it." From this we understand that in a case when it is necessary to inform someone for a justified reason, it is acceptable. This includes the permission to inform parents and relatives.

Igros Kodesh, Volume 7, p. 303

Husband should not be in the delivery room

The Rebbe stated clearly that the husband should not be present in the delivery room during the actual delivery of the baby.

Teshuvus u'Beurim, p. 445

Say chapters of Tehillim during the delivery

The Rebbe recommends, based on what was done during the birth of the Rebbe Mahrash, that the husband say the following chapters of *Tehillim* at the time the wife is delivering the baby:

Chapters: 1-4, 20-24, 33, 47, 72, 86, 90, 91, 104, 112, 113-150.

Sefer HaToldos Admur MahRash, prepared by Rebbe, p. 5

Delaying chasuna leads to breakdown in tznius

Your doubts about finalizing the wedding as planned are a result of your having delayed the wedding date to months in the distant future. Since, as it is planned currently, your wedding date is not right away, you fail the challenge of *tznius*. You should change the wedding date to be right away instead of several months in the future; this will reduce the breakdown of *tznius* and cause you to remove the doubts and consummate the wedding as planned.

Beis Moshiach, #70, p. 9

7
JEWISH NAMES

Channels personal energy

Generally speaking, the giving of a name is a great responsibility. The name is a channel which draws down Hashem's positive energy to the person or object being called by that name.

Igros Kodesh, Volume 5, p. 123

Usually the emphasis on a name as explained in Talmud, chasidus, and Kabbalah, refers to the first name(s), not the familial name. However, there were occasions when the Rebbe did explain the significance of certain family names.

Name, job, and character

In 1947 the Rebbe traveled to France to greet his mother. At a farbrengen in Paris, he asked all participants to tell him their first names. He then explained the association between each one's name, job, and character.

Yimei Melech, Volume 3, p. 980

This approach was seen clearly in the Rebbe's public farbrengens. He would explain the significance of a talmudic sage's name as it relates to the particular comment he makes. At times the Rebbe shared the association of certain chasid's names as it pertained to their life's work for Yiddishkeit. The Rebbe's underlying principle in all this was that you are who your name is and, more importantly, if one identifies with his name, he understands how all the energy Hashem gives him comes because of his name and through his name.

Who decides a child's name

Based on the teachings of the *Rishonim*, their custom was that the first child's name was the choice of the father, the second the mother, the third the father, etc. Unless there is a specific custom otherwise, it is my opinion to follow this as a general rule.

Igros Kodesh, Volume 5, p. 123

Parents should agree

Someone wrote the Rebbe that the name of their child is so-and-so. The Rebbe responded that surely this name was agreed upon by both him and his wife.

Igros Kodesh, Volume 14, p. 256

Do not mix in

The Rebbe, when asked what name to give to a child, would generally refrain from responding. He said that, based on the teachings of the Arizal, the name of a child is decided by heavenly wisdom given to the parents at the time of naming the child. The Rebbe said that he does not interfere with this decision.

Response to author

I had that in mind

However, there were times when people chose a name and told the Rebbe what it was and he acknowledged it. For example, a *chasid* told the Rebbe he gave his son the name "Yosef Yitzchak." The Rebbe responded:

I was glad to read of the name you choose for your son...the name is the exact one I was thinking of.

Igros Kodesh, Volume 13, p. 27

Name a girl at first chance

The Rebbe encouraged that a girl be named at the first opportunity, which is the first day the Torah is read after the girl is born. In Chabad this the custom; the Rebbe wished that it become not only a Chabad custom, but that all Jews follow in the same vein.

The Rebbe's reasons were three-fold:

1. The name of a person is her life force, and therefore the sooner she is named, the better.

2. Moshiach's arrival depends on the completion of all souls entering their designated bodies; it is understood that as soon as this happens, the time of Moshiach's coming moves closer. The soul's connection to the body is through the letters of the name. It could be that this particular child is the last one left in the "storehouse" of souls waiting to enter the body, culminating with Moshiach's arrival.

3. Since a woman does not need a circumcision, since it is considered as though she is born circumcised (*Avoda Zora*, 26a), her holy soul enters the body when

she is born. Possibly this entrance comes at the time when the girl is given her name.

Hisva'adiyus, 5750, Volume 3, p. 364; Likutei Sichos,
Volume 14, p. 250

Baby naming before bris

In select cases when a child was ill and the parents requested a *brocha* from the Rebbe, he told them to decide a name for the child, even though it was before the *bris*, and that they should let him know the name so that he could pray for the child. Once, in the winter of 1984, a boy was born with serious medical complications. The father met the Rebbe face-to-face and asked him for a *brocha*. The Rebbe responded:

"What is his name?"

The father replied that because of the medical condition, the child had not yet received his *bris* and he had no name. The Rebbe said, "Speak to your wife via telephone and both of you decide on a name and let me know."

Hiskashrus, Volume 77 , p. 11

The name Avrohom

A boy was born *Shabbos parshas Chaya Sara*. The father wanted to name him "Avrohom," but the mother objected. They wrote the Rebbe, and he wrote back:

He (Avrohom) lived many good, healthy years, was wealthy, etc. What else do you want?!

Hiskashrus, Volume 77, p. 12

Naming after a living person

Among Sephardim, when a father names a child after his living father, the grandfather of the new baby boy, it is a means of showing respect to the grandparent. Ashkenazim are careful not to do this, but rather to give a name after a deceased relative.

Hisva'adiyus, 5743, Volume 2, p. 760

The names of the Previous Rebbe and Tzemach Tzedek

On *Shabbos Breishis*, 5715, the Rebbe said that for all those who needed a blessing to have children, Hashem should bless them with healthy children who should be named after the Previous Rebbe, Yosef Yitzchak, or after the Tzemach Tzedek, Menachem Mendel.

Sichos Kodesh, 5715, p. 69

Combining names: Yes or no?

The Rebbe, in the early years of his leadership, said that the Previous Rebbe hesitated to combine names. When a name is given, it should be after one person.

Yimei Breishis, p. 100

However, in *Chodesh Sivan* of 5751 the Rebbe wrote to a *chasid* who wanted to name his son after one of the Lubavitcher Rebbeim, but his father objected and wanted him to give the name of his father, the boy's grandfather. The Rebbe responded:

"He should do what his father wants, especially since this occurs after the festival of *Shavuos* when the Torah was given from anew (as we discussed just recently), in which we read "*Kabed Es Avicho*" (respect your father)."

Then the Rebbe added, "You can add other names after your father's name choice."

Hiskashrus, Volume 77, p. 12

Name makes you responsible

In 1983, the Alexander Rebbe and his son visited the Rebbe. Towards the end of *yechidus* he presented his son to the Rebbe and told him that his son's name is Shneur Zalman. The Rebbe said that his name obligates him to reveal his potential into the actual.

This responsibility is given to him from the time of *Har Sinai*, and one has been sworn to fulfill it.

Bzel Chochma, p. 197

The meaning of Chaya Mushka

The Rebbe explained that this name refers to the activation of both inner and outer energy. Chaya comes from the word *chayos* (energy), specifically referring to penetrated, inner, digested energy. *Mushka* is a type of fragrance which, according to certain people, is the 11th fragrance of the *ketoras* (incense) used in the holy temple. Spiritually, it represents the peripheral powers of the soul which are given to a person.

(See my book, *Demystifying the Mystical*, chapter 4, for detailed explanation of these terms).

Sefer HaSichos, 5752, Volume 2, p. 352

Chapter 7 / Jewish Names

Changing names

The Rebbe, in many different letters throughout his leadership, has advocated minimizing the changing of a Hebrew name given to a person at birth or bris. Some examples:

One should not add or change a name without an important reason.

Igros Kodesh, Volume 8, p. 318

To change or add a name follow a Rav's opinion (since there are different customs). Generally why do you want to change?

Kfar Chabad, Volume 656, p. 57

In regard to the names, it is not understood why you wish to change them; your name and your wife's name are holy names.

Igros Kodesh, Volume 20, p. 165

You write there are several people in your community that have forgotten their Jewish names, and you want to give them new names during the *mesheberach* ceremony (*"Mesheberach"* means "who blesses," referring to *Hashem* Who blesses the person. This blessing is said during the Torah service).

You do not write the pressing reason to do this. Surely you must know some of these peoples' names by looking at their birth certificates or asking their parents.

Igros Kodesh, Volume 6, p. 154

The name to counter cancer

A woman told the Rebbe that her daughter had cancer and she asked the Rebbe for a *brocha* that her daughter be healthy. She also asked the Rebbe if she should change her daughter's name.

The Rebbe responded:

Add the name "Gila" or "Simcha." (*Both names mean "joy" or "happiness."*)

Zoreah Tzedakos, p. 119

Changing name chosen by grandparent

You inform me that your daughter was given a name by her grandmother and you want to change it. Since this name was chosen and given during the *mesheberach* ceremony, do not change the name; rather, add another name to it. You can do this because the original name was given without your consent.

Igros Kodesh, Volume 8, p. 191

Reverting to a previous name

You ask about reverting to a name you had in the past because you are having a difficulty and feel that maybe it is because of the new name.

This wonders me. Why change your current name, which is a Hebrew name?

Igros Kodesh, Volume 17, p. 38

It is not clear from the letter if his previous name was a Jewish one or not.

Calling yourself by Hebrew name

The year 5748 was a *Hakhel* year, and the Rebbe wanted a list of all participants in *Hakhel* programs. He said:

Incidentally, there is an advantage to get all those names on this list, because even those people who do not normally use their Jewish names will be asked for them to be recorded onto the list. This will reveal to them and others their Jewish names, as explained in *Midrash* regarding the virtue of not changing our names when we were in Egypt.

Sefer HaSichos, 5748, Volume 1, p. 21, fn 106

The name Marta

A woman asked the Rebbe to suggest to her a Jewish name. Her name was Marten (French name). The Rebbe responded:

"Sara is a Jewish name. What is your sister's name?"

She responded:

"Sara."

The Rebbe said:

"Continue calling her Sara. You should be called Marta because this name is found in the *gemora* Marta ben Bisus."

Hiskashrus, Volume 77, p. 15

The names Collete, Algeria, Duna

A French lady passed by the Rebbe in line to receive a dollar for *tzedaka*. Her French name was Collete. She asked the Rebbe for a Jewish name. The Rebbe told her she should choose the name *Keli* or *Kela*.

To another person whose name was *Algeria*, the Rebbe said that she be called *Brocha*.

To yet another whose name was Duna, the Rebbe suggested *Adina*.

Kfar Chabad, Volume 705

Rebbe's suggested names

It was the Rebbe's custom (see my upcoming book, *The Seven Chabad-Lubavitch Rebbes*, the chapter on the Rebbe, for detailed explanation), on Sunday mornings, to distribute dollar bills to people who visited him, thus making them messengers for giving tzedaka. Some of these people did not have Jewish names and asked the Rebbe for his recommendation. These are some of names he suggested. We must remember that one's Jewish name is their life force; the Rebbe's suggestion applies to the individual who asked, based on the Rebbe's insight into the spiritual "energy" of that person's soul. Nevertheless, a person who has any of the following secular names can look into himself and see if the Rebbe's suggestion also fits his own character and personality. If one does adopt the Rebbe's suggestion, even though it was said to another person, one can incorporate that energy in a most positive way.

Yivgeni-Avroham or Yitzchak; Robert-Reuven; Brian-Baruch; Frank-Efrayim; Iris-Uriya; Rima-Rina; Machnes-Machla or Machne; Junt-Yona; Mishel-Michel; Inge-Rivka;

Claire-Kreina; Ninesi-Pnina; Claudia-Malka; Marian-Miriam; Leda-Leah or Malka; Nigema-Nechama; Debra-Devora; Pardos-Adina; Yanina-Yitzchaka; Irene-Ilana; Lili-Leah; Flora-Shoshana; Donald-Dan or Dovid.

Zoreah Tzedakos, NY 5753, pp. 129-131

Names of goyim

In general, for a Jewish person making a blessing for healing, the person's first name(s) and mother's names are mentioned. After one's passing, when making a prayer for him, the person's (deceased) father's name is mentioned. Several times, when people requested a blessing for gentiles who were still alive, the Rebbe requested to know their father's name.

Hiskashrus, Volume 77, p. 16

Name after one who died in war

In regard to your question whether it is proper to name a child after a father who perished in war, the fact is there were several people with that name, not just your father. Therefore, if both parents are in agreement, you can give that name, and may he live long, good years.

Igros Kodesh, Volume 12, p. 434

Remedy for long life

The name "Ben Tzion" is a remedy to live a long life.

Igros Kodesh, Volume 11, p. 73

Order of names

The order of the names demonstrates the quality one over the other.

Sefer HaSichos, 5750, Volume 4, p.

Publicizing author's and contributors' names

It is customary to print the names of those who dedicated the book by paying for its printing. It is also worthwhile to print the names of all those who helped in preparing the book for print, such as the publisher, editors, binders, etc.

The author's name is very important to be printed in the book for several reasons:

1. Our sages say it is a mitzvah to publicize one who does a mitzvah.

2. This is particularly true of an author who puts into his book much more than what is written. (*He puts his essence into his writing. This essence is not necessarily seen in print*).

3. In regard to education, the publication of the author's name is more relevant, because the students who will read this book are impacted more when they know that their teacher wrote the book. It will add to their *yiras shomayim*.

Sichas 20 *Kislev*, 5737, and *Sefer Hechel Menachem*, Volume 1, p. 103

Whispering Rebbe's name into ear

The Previous Rebbe's name was whispered into the ear of a woman who fainted. She woke up from her faint and resumed her normal routine. The Rebbe explained that since his father-in-law was a collective soul, she being part of his soul, the mention of his name aroused her from her illness.

Likutei Sichos, Volume 2, p. 516

8
BUSINESS, OCCUPATIONS, INVESTMENTS

Picture your Rebbe's face

From time to time picture to yourself your Rebbe's face this Jew's teacher was the Minchas Elozor, the Munkatcher Rebbe, and attempt to help others who need spiritual guidance. Hashem will give you *parnasa* in a big way, in all physical and spiritual matters.

Igros Kodesh, Volume 21, p. 135

Seemingly this person asked the Rebbe for a brocha for parnasa. The interesting factor here is that the Rebbe normally advised people to picture the Previous Rebbe's face. Here, he instead tells him to bring to mind his own Rebbe's image!

Pushkas in business

Someone asked a *brocha* for *parnasa*. The Rebbe asked him if he had a *pushka* in his place of business. He said no, but he had one at home. The Rebbe said that, in order to have success in his business, he should put an additional *pushka* in his place of business.

Zoreah Tzedakos, p. 121

Closing business Friday after midday

Someone asked the Rebbe for a *brocha* that his business go well. The Rebbe told him to make sure that there be the proper *Shabbos* adherence at the store. He said to the Rebbe that there is, because the store is closed on *Shabbos*.

The Rebbe said the meaning of the word "proper" implies not only *Shabbos*, but also Friday from midday on. This is the "proper" way of adhering to *Shabbos*.

Zoreah Tzedakos, p. 121

Profits of Shabbos to non-observant partner

In reply to your question as to whether you should purchase a business together with a Jewish partner who does not observe *Shabbos*, in which the profits from the sales made on *Shabbos* would go only to him and you would not have any benefit financially from the *Shabbos* sales.

I strongly suggest you refrain from doing this,

because you surely know that money made based on the desecration of *Shabbos* not only will go to waste, but more so, it will cause other money to be lost as well. Why would you, as a businessperson, want to buy a business which will more than likely lose money?!

Igros Kodesh, Volume 4, p. 270

Although there are halachic ways of permitting such an arrangement, it seems from the Rebbe's reply that it is better to stay away from anything that sounds, feels, and smells like chilul Shabbos. Before a person does or does not buy such a business, he must consult a Rav.

Business partners get it in writing

Based on the conduct of our holy sages, it is best if all the details agreed upon should be in writing, so that there will no doubts or confusion as to what was agreed upon and what was not. This will accomplish peace between yourselves, not only in day-to-day activities so that a *chasid* will not be accused of any wrongdoing but, more importantly, deep inner peace coming from the depth of your hearts.

Igros Kodesh, Volume 11, Letter 3778

Horse trainer

The Rebbe said to a horse trainer that his horses should have much success in their races. "They should run as they are supposed to." The Rebbe told the horse trainer's wife that she should have success even with horse matters!

Zoreah Tzedakos, p. 141

Horse betting

You write that some people are encouraging your son to bet on horses as a means of employment.

It is understood that this should not be done, because it is a sure way to lose money, G-d forbid.

May Hashem grant him *parnasa* in a peaceful and kosher way.

Igros Kodesh, Volume 9, p. 229

Not being partner in business if not knowledgeable

Someone asked the Rebbe if he should become a partner in a business in which he had no knowledge or experience.

The Rebbe told him that, since he has no understanding of the makings of this business, he must solely rely on his partner's information and trust. He will have no way of controlling the situation because he does not know the intricacies of this business. It is highly questionable if it makes sense to do this, unless he can arrange to have an expert in this business represent him and can have this expert be involved throughout the entire venture, not just initially. Realistically, it is very difficult to find such a person. Therefore the Rebbe did not agree with the entire idea and his recommendation was to stay away.

Nelcha b'Urchosav, p. 205

Journalist

I wonder why you do not use the opportunity that you have as a journalist to disseminate information about Torah and *mitzvos*, including the teachings of *chasidus*. The so-called excuse that your editor would not appreciate it can be easily refuted. When one wants a pay raise he does not say, how can I argue with my editor? Why? Because he needs the money. So also, in regard to spiritual matters, one can and should write about spirituality, regardless of what the editor's wishes are.

Sefer Hechel Menachem, Volume 3, p. 103

No such thing as a "professional" chasid

Based on the teachings of *chasidus*, there is no such thing as a "professional" *chasid* or professional chasidism. If one see in the chasidic movement "professionalism," he is not a *chasid*. *Chasidus* is based on an inner passionate bond to Hashem, causing a internal transformation within the person.

Sefer Hechel Menachem, Volume 3, p. 120

> The Rebbe is explaining that chasidus is not to be seen as another profession, similar to other formal, organized professions. This does not mean that to be a chasid, one should not have a profession, or that using chasidic knowledge to enhance one's work is unacceptable. On the contrary, the Baal Shem Tov teaches that one should incorporate his chasidus into mundane affairs. The Rebbe is simply saying that chasidus is not something one does as a professional; rather, it is total transformation of the self.

Investing in Israel

Several years ago, a chairman of the Israeli Bonds organization asked the Rebbe for advice. The problem was that when Jews were asked to contribute financially towards the needs of the newly arrived Russian Jews in Israel, they say they do not want to give because they are not interested in this cause.

The Rebbe told him that Israel is one of the safest places in the world. Whoever invests his money into Israel by buying real estate, or by investing into projects or organizations in Israel, is investing into one of the best banks that exist in our time.

Zoreah Tzedakos, p. 51

What is a Chabad Rebbe's job?

As with all Chabad-Lubavitch Rebbes, the first principle is his true subservience to Hashem. Since he is a Rebbe, it is his primary mission to lead and support the people in Torah and mitzvos, (beginning with strengthening their faith in Hashem and following the code of Jewish law), to be a living example (to the point of mesiras nefesh b'poel, i.e., in actuality) of Torah and mitzvos. It is self understood that anything that can be interpreted in a negative way the Rebbe refrains from doing.

After all of the above, what follows is his personal life. In addition, fundamental to his personal life is that it is not allowed to affect his primary communal life in any way at all.

Nelcha b'Urchosav, p. 230

9
MITZVOS AND JEWISH CUSTOMS

Kiddush Levana sanctification of the moon

One should be meticulous in observing the mitzvah of *kiddush levana* (this is the monthly ritual in which we say prayers comparing the Jewish nation to the moon. Just as the moon goes from being very small to large and beautiful, so, too, the Jewish people are in numbers very small, but through following Hashem's will are very large).

This diligence and effort in performing the mitzvah should be done with wearing beautiful clothing (i.e., Shabbos garments, if the ritual is done *motzoei Shabbos* as is preferred and if the calendar cycle allows it; or if done during a weekday, nice, clean weekday clothing), in the public street, with as big of a crowd as possible and it should be done at the proper time based on guidance of the code of Jewish law. When doubtful, consult a Rav.

The overall intent when performing the mitzvah should be to hasten the arrival of Moshiach by our beseeching Hashem to send Moshiach, as we recite at the conclusion of the *kiddush levana* prayer: "They request G-d their G-d and Dovid their king, Amen."

Sichas Parshas Noach, 5752

Soldiers wearing ammunition on Shabbos

You ask whether you are permitted to wear your ammunition or helmet on *Shabbos*. When you are instructed to go on an offensive attack, or if you are attacked, ordained rabbis have already ruled it is permissible.

I suggest you get hold of the *Sefer Machne Israel*, authored by the Chofetz Chaim, which addresses many questions that are relevant to soldiers.

Igros Kodesh, Volume 7, p. 220

Eating carob on Lag b'Omer

It is customary to eat carob on the day the great sage Rabbi Shimon Bar Yochai passed on. This is because the *gemora* says Hashem made a miracle, a carob tree and a well of water appeared in the cave in which he and his son were hiding from the Roman terrors.

I remember that in my father's house on *Lag b'Omer* we ate carob, although it was very difficult to obtain and was very expensive to buy. Only on this day did we eat carob.

Hisva'adiyus, 5742, Volume 3, p. 1395

Immersing in the mikva before visiting the cemetery

I have not seen my father-in-law visit the cemetery on *Tishe b'Av*. The probable reason is that one is not permitted to immerse in the *mikva* on this day, so he did not go to the cemetery, which is a holy place.

Some people will go to the cemetery, standing outside without going in, and look at the grave (s) from the outside. However, I also did not see my father-in-law do that on *Tishe b'Av*. The possible explanation is, based on the statements made in different *seforim*, that just looking at a grave creates some connection. Therefore, without being able to go to the *mikva*, he would not even stand on the outside and look at the grave.

Igros Kodesh, Volume 11, p. 307

There are other customs pertaining to the visiting the cemetery on Tishe b'Av. The Rebbe is explaining the possible reason why his father-in-law did not go.

Chazan should review, yearly, the meaning of the words

Surely you are aware of the instruction given by our holy *Rebbeim* that a *chazan*, throughout the year but more importantly on the high holidays, should review the prayers, know the actual translation of the words, and be motivated by the chasidic insights associated with them.

Although one has done so the previous year, each year a *chazan* should do all of the above again.

Igros Kodesh, Volume 6, p. 324, & Volume 11, p. 416

Forgot to daven

First the way to rectify missing davening is to make a firm resolution that from here on it will never happen again, and to regret letting it happen in the past. Additionally, become an expert in the laws of davening that are necessary to one's life. Those laws which are not relevant to each person, but only to the *chazan*, are not the ones in which you should become an expert.

Yagdil Torah, Israel, Volume 4, p. 1804

Torah that fell

The adults who saw the way the Torah fell, although it was wrapped with its mantle, should fast 4 half-days, and the students who witnessed the falling should fast an additional half day. All should be careful in saying the weekly parsha twice and the Targum once, known as *shenayim mikra vechod targum*. One frank (French coin) should be given daily to the Talmud Torah's *tzedaka* fund.

Igros Kodesh, Volume 7, p. 83

Tikun for having child from gentile

As part of a corrective measure, you are to immediately get involved, with complete and total dedication to the point of *mesiras nefesh*, in the field of Jewish education. Each morning before davening, give *tzedaka* to an institution which educates children in the spirit of *Yiddishkeit*.

Chapter 9 / Mitzvos and Jewish Customs

Every day after davening, including *Shabbos* and *Yom Tov*, say the daily portion of *Tehillim*, as divided by the days of the month. Additionally, do your part in reaching out to Jews are not yet observant and bring them closer to Hashem.

Igros Kodesh, Volume 15, p. 325

Gentile might have touched wine

Someone wrote the Rebbe that during a wedding he possibly distributed wine that was touched by a non-Jew, rendering it invalid for consumption by a Jew. This law is known as *yain nesech*.

Although you write it is doubtful whether the gentile actually touched the wine, I suggest you give to *tzedaka* the equivalent of the cost of 73 meals. The money does not have to given all at once but can be distributed until the upcoming *Rosh HaShana*.

Igros Kodesh, Volume 12, p. 408

Afraid Upsherinish will cause cold

You write that your son's ritual three-year-old haircutting is supposed to be in the winter, and you are concerned that the change from having hair to not having hair during the winter can cause him to catch a bad cold. Because of this you want to postpone the *upsherinish*.

My opinion is that you do not delay the scheduled *upsherinish* date, based on my father-in-law's words. The implication is that when the child's hair is cut and *peyos* (halachic side locks) are noticeable on the child an additional amount of holiness is added to the child's soul. This being so, why do you want to delay this level of holiness from entering the soul?

On the other hand, it is not necessary to give your child a complete haircut during the winter if you are afraid he will catch a bad cold. You can leave over lots of hair, as long as the *peyos* are noticeable. Later, when the weather becomes nicer, you can cut the remaining hair.

Igros Kodesh, Volume 14, p. 313

It must be stated clearly that the Rebbe's suggestion is only because this woman was overly concerned and was about to postpone the upsherinish from its proper date. However, one should endeavor to have the complete faith in Hashem that, when performing a mitzvah or a Jewish custom, no harm will come from it, and a complete haircut should be given. But again, as the Rebbe says, there is no requirement to cut most of the hair at the third birthday, as long as peyos are noticeable.

Upsherinish customs

The Rebbe said and did the following to a Lubavitcher boy at his Upsherinish:

1. *Cut some hair near the child's right side locks (peyos).*

2. *The* shiur *of the peyos is to let the hair grow a little below the bone.*

3. *We begin teaching the child the* alef-beis *from the cover page of the* Tanya.

4. *In order to show the child that Torah is sweet, take a toothpick and dip it into honey. Put a drop onto the cover*

page of the Tanya, *in such a manner that none of the cover page will get ruined, G-d forbid.*

5. *When teaching the boy alef-beis from the* Tanya, *let him lick the honey off the page so that he will see that Torah is indeed sweet.*

Teshura Katz, 20th Cheshvan, 5758

Make chasidisher farbrengen at Bar-Mitzvah

In response to your question as to whether to make a big public event for your son's bar-mitzvah or a small quiet get-together: Seemingly, since at the age of thirteen a boy becomes responsible to fulfill Torah and *mitzvos*, it is appropriate to celebrate it in a festive, public manner. This was true even in the past, when *Yiddishkeit* was vibrant. How much more so in our day and age, when Judaism lacks the observance as in the past, is it desirable to seize any opportunity to strengthen Torah and *mitzvos*.

My intent is not that one should spend lots of money on the affair; rather, the public event should consist of spiritual quality, the way a chasidic Torah celebration is. By having the bar-mitzvah in the aforementioned manner, the participants will wish the bar-mitzvah boy that he should be a *chasid, yirei shomayim*, and *lamden*.

According to a well-known saying of our holy *Rebbeim*, "what a *chasidisher* farbrengen can accomplish even the angel Michoel cannot accomplish."

Igros Kodesh, Volume 10, p. 376

Bar-Mitzvah trip

The idea of a bar-mitzvah is that a child becomes an adult, obligating him in all *mitzvos*. This responsibility does not correspond with taking pleasure trips as a reward for becoming bar-mitzvah. On the contrary, a pleasure trip is associated with freedom, the opposite of *kabbalas ol malchus shomayim*, the yoke of firmly accepting Hashem's will.

This acceptance in no way contradicts the joyful attitude the bar-mitzvah boy needs to have because he merited to be a son and servant of the Almighty King. We learn this from the very first bar-mitzvah recorded in the *midrash* of Yitzchak *avinu*. Avrohom made a big feast for his son's bar-mitzvah. Yet we find that we are obligated to recite *tachnun* (supplication prayer) on the day of the bar-mitzvah. The festive mood does not exempt one from supplication, because bar-mitzvah is not a day that we rest from work. Rather, it is a day that we increase our work towards Hashem by doing more *mitzvos* and learning more Torah.

Sefer Hechel Menachem, Volume 3, pp. 48-49

This letter was written to the Chabad Youth Organization in Israel. They wanted to bring a group of bar-mitzvah boys, who were war-orphans, to visit the Rebbe and other sites in New York.

Celebrating a deceased child's birthday

It is appropriate to celebrate the day of a deceased child's birthday by doing all the normal customs associated with a birthday and giving *tzedaka* in his memory.

The amount of *tzedaka* should correspond to the numerical equivalent of the child's name. A chasidic farbrengen should be made in conjunction with the birthday.

Sefer Hechel Menachem, Volume 3, pp. 55-56

Chasidic Bas-Mitzvah celebration

Do not make a bas-mitzvah celebration the way a bar-mitzvah is celebrated. Those who do it that way are attempting to emulate the boys' event. The way to celebrate the significant day in which a girl becomes obligated to do her *mitzvos* is to make a modest event in her school as a birthday party, and her parents should buy her a beautiful present.

Sha'arei Minhag v'Halacha, Volume 2, pp. 311

Tikun for forgetting to put on Rabbeinu Tam's Tefillin

Become an expert in the practical laws of *Tefillin* and in the first 12 chapters of *Tanya*. The importance of knowing *Tanya* by heart is explained in my father-in-law's famous talk. *Printed in* Likutei Dibburim, *volume 4, page 712, Sefer HaSichos* Admur Ma'aryatz, *1928-1931, p. 168.*

Sefer Hechel Menachem, Volume 3, p. 41

Tikun for lighting Shabbos candles late

I received your letter informing me that you lit your *Shabbos* candles at the wrong time based on the erroneous time listed in the newspaper.

I suggest the following:

1. Give $7.02 to tzedaka over the course of several weeks. It is preferable if this is done *Erev Shabbos* before you light the candles. 702 is the gematria (numerical equivalent) of the Hebrew word "Shabbos."

2. Study the laws of *Shabbos* from the *Kitzur Shulchan Aruch*, which is also readily available in English, making it easier for you to study.

3. Influence several other ladies to learn these laws together with you.

4. Completely remove your thoughts from this issue (being harsh on herself).

5. Check the *mezuzos* of your entire house.

Igros Kodesh, Volume 5, p. 126

Tikunim for disgracing shul and Sefer Torah

1. On the day which the disgraced Torah scrolls will be buried, the writing of a new Torah scroll should begin. If possible, the writing activity should be done as close to the holy ark as possible.

2. A class of pre-bar-mitzvah children should learn during their regular class hours in the *shul* for thirty days, instead of studying in their regular classrooms.

3. There should be at least one *minyon* daily until after the holidays. (This desecration happened in the summer).

4. More Torah books should be brought to the *shul*, replacing the ones that were disgraced and ruined. The amount of *seforim* brought should outnumber the *seforim* which were damaged.

Chapter 9 / Mitzvos and Jewish Customs

5. An increase of *pushkas* (charity boxes) should be added to the *shul*.

6. The establishment of a free-loan society should be made, and on the day of the above ceremonies the first free loan should be given.

7. On this *Shabbos* (the first *Shabbos* following the desecration), representatives of other *shuls* in Yerusholayim (this happened in Jerusalem) should *daven* in your *shul*.

8. This *Shabbos* there should be an increase in the public classes given in the *shul*.

9. There should be an increase in the third *Shabbos* meal activity, including the recitation of a *ma'amor chasidus*.

10. It is my hope that you exert yourselves and find someone who has a child that needs to be circumcised on this *Shabbos*. Convince him to do it in your *shul*, and the *shul* should contribute to the expenses of the *bris mitzvah* meal.

Sefer Hechel Menachem, Volume 2, pp. 41-42

This was written to the organizers of a Chabad shul in Jerusalem after holy books and sifrei Torah were abused, disgracing their shul. The Rebbe suggested that these 10 things be done immediately so that the very first Shabbos following the catastrophe should be a rectification of the problem.

Melave Malka or Mesibas Shabbos as Bas-Mitzvah celebration

The bas-mitzvah event can be in the form of a *melave malka*, or a *mesibas Shabbos*.

Sha'arei Minhag v'Halacha, Volume 2, p. 312

Birthday customs and practices

1. Be called to the Torah for an *aliya* on the *Shabbos* which precedes the birthday. If the birthday is on Monday or Thursday, one should get an *aliya* on that day as well.

2. Give additional *tzedaka* before *shachris* and *mincha* on the birthday. If it is on a *Shabbos* or holiday, when it is forbidden to handle money, it should be given on *erev Shabbos* or *erev Yom Tov*. (Even better is to give *tzedaka* the day after *Shabbos* and *Yom Tov* as well).

3. Increase davening through having more intent, meditating on the greatness of Hashem, etc. Say at least one of the five books of *Tehillim*. Preferably, the entire book of *Tehillim* should be said.

4. Study your new chapter in *Tehillim* corresponding to the age of your upcoming birthday.

5. Learn an additional *shiur* in Torah, both in *nigla* and *chasidus*. This should be done after one studies *Chumash*, *Tehillim*, and the daily portion of *Tanya*.

6. Study by heart any *ma'amor* which interests you. The study should involve your essence. If possible, study an entire *ma'amor* or at least some part of a *ma'amor*. The *ma'amor* should be recited among a group of people on the birthday itself or at the first opportunity, especially the *Shabbos* following the birthday, during *shalosh seudas*.

7. Bring the image of the Rebbe's face to your mind, picture a *yechidus* you had with the Rebbe, the question you asked and the answer he gave, and following this study some of his teachings.

Chapter 9 / Mitzvos and Jewish Customs

8. Reach out to another Jew and bring him closer to Hashem by showing love for him.

9. Isolate yourself for a while, sometime during the 24-hour birthday period. During that time, think about those things in your life, which need improvement, and make firm positive resolutions about yourself in the upcoming year.

10. Take upon yourself an additional specific *hidur* (good custom). You can begin by adding another regular *shiur* in *chasidus*. Since one's birthday is his individual *Rosh HaShana*, therefore, just as on *Rosh HaShana*, it is appropriate to take upon oneself a new custom, so, too, this is proper for a person's personal *Rosh HaShana*, his birthday.

11. Arrange a farbrengen with your family members, friends, and acquaintances. At the farbrengen, thanks to Hashem should be given through *simcha* of Torah and mitzvah. If possible, the *brocha* "*Shehecheyanu*" should be recited on a new fruit or new garment.

Sefer HaSichos, 5748, Volume 2, p. 406

Birthday celebration for one-year-old

When a child reaches his first birthday, the parents should do the customs associated with one's birthday, such as giving *tzedaka* and learning Torah in the merit of the child. Most important should be the meditation that Hashem gave them such a great loan, by having a soul enter a holy body in which they have the opportunity and obligation to educate and teach the right Torah way, enabling the precious loan to be a shining light.

Hisva'adiyus, 5742, Volume 4, p. 2190

Cornerstone ceremony

The ceremony in which a stone is placed in the ground, symbolizing the foundation of a building, has its source in Torah.

Based on the words of our holy sages that Hashem created the world by looking into Torah, so also, when one establishes a building, it should begin with words of Torah. The following are several things which should be done at the ceremony:

1. Words of Torah should be said before the cornerstone is laid. Particularly, these words of Torah should be associated to building a home, community, etc. Many of these explanations are found in Chabad *chasidus ma'amorim* on the verse "*mizmor shir chanukas habayis.*"

2. The actual placing of the cornerstone should be done by children under bar- and bas-mitzvah, because our sages teach that their breath is pure of sin and the world stands because of them.

3. The actual stone used as the symbolic foundation should be a natural one, not one carved out by some craftsman. Of course later on, after the ceremony, other bricks that are man-made can be added. The spiritual reason for this is that the beginning of every building and thing is possible only because of Hashem giving one the power to accomplish it. A natural rock is symbolic of this, since it comes from Hashem. However, a brick that was carved out beautifully by man symbolically denotes man's part, as though man were the foundation, G-d forbid.

Igros Kodesh, Volume 19, p. 211

Reciting ma'amor at chanukas habayis

At your dedication celebrating your new home, make a *chasidisher* farbrengen at which time a *ma'amor chasidus* will be said. Doing this will be beneficial materially and spiritually.

Sefer HaMinhagim, p. 81

Sleeping with tzitzis

To avoid fears during your sleep, be careful to recite *Shema* before going to sleep, wear a *talis katan* (*tzitzis*) the entire night, and make sure the *tzitzis* are kosher, with each corner of the *talis katan* having 8 strings. Additionally, on days other than *Shabbos* and *Yom Tov*, when writing is permitted, before you go to sleep, write down those things that you missed learning in your studies during the day because your mind was elsewhere. This way you will be able to make it up the next day.

Igros Kodesh, Volume 13, p. 29

Kissing the mezuzah at night

In every Jewish home parents are careful to have their children kiss the *mezuzah* of their room before going to sleep. The portion of *Shema* is written on the *mezuzah* and the words "Hashem Echad" will be engraved into the children, guarding them and everything else in their room from problems, as explained in the *Zohar*.

Hisva'adiyus, 5747, Volume 2, p. 647

Stopping the pulling of hairs from beard

Start wearing gloves on your hands, so that if you have an urge to pull out hair from your beard you will not do it. This is practical but helpful advice. The advice that was given in the past was to smear mustard onto the beard, causing one not to touch the beard. However, this advice is more expensive!

Zoreah Tzedakos, p. 139

Kashrus standards Benedictine brand

I am directed to acknowledge receipt of your letter, in which you inquire as to the *kashrus* of a certain liqueur.

May we state in reply, firstly, that your question should be directed to a Rov whose function it is to *pasken shaalos* of this nature.

Secondly, there is no basis for the assumption that any particular liqueur has any particular significance to a particular movement, either in its use or abstention. Even where a thing is permissible for consumption, anyone who desires to take a "stricter" view and abstain from it may certainly do so, and it will in no way affect his relationship to the particular movement.

Judging by the tenor of your letter, the opportunity is taken to express the hope that you have regular appointed times for the study of Torah, both *nigla* as well as the inner aspects of the Torah, namely *chasidus*, bearing in mind that all matters of holiness should be on the ascendancy.

Teshura Nagel, Lag B'Omer, 5757, p. 103

> This letter was written to a yeshiva student at the Gateshead yeshiva. The student had complaints that people of the Lubavitcher movement drink the liqueur called "Benedictine." He questioned its kashrus. After the student received the letter, he told some Chabad member in London that he was most touched, not by the Rebbe's response about the liqueur but more so by the Rebbe's request that he affix regular time to Torah study, because it had been more than three years since he had opened a Jewish sefer to learn!

Overdoing grief

You must make every effort to regain the proper state of mind, despite the pain. You should remember the teaching and instruction of the Torah, which is called *Toras Chayim* (Guide in Life) and *Toras Emes* (the Torah of Truth), meaning that what it teaches is not just to ease the mind, but the actual truth. Thus, the Torah, taking into account human nature/feelings in a case of bereavement, and the need to provide an outlet for the natural feelings of sorrow and grief, prescribes a set of regulations and periods of mourning.

At the same time, the Torah sets limits in terms of the duration of the periods of mourning and the appropriate expression, such as *shiva* (the first seven days), *shloshim* (thirty days), etc. If one extends the intensity of mourning that is appropriate for *shiva* into *shloshim*, it is not proper, for although *shloshim* is part of the overall mourning period, it is so to a lesser degree. And since the Torah says that it is not proper to overdo it, it does no good for the *neshomo* of the dear departed. On the contrary, it is painful for the *neshomo* to see that it is the cause for the conduct that is not in keeping with the instructions of the Torah.

Letter, *Tammuz*, 5743

10. MISCELLANEOUS

Dream interpretation

A woman told the Rebbe she dreamt that a Torah scroll surrounded the Rebbe; she said to him "you have the *Shechina*," and the Rebbe said to her the words "almonds, almonds." What is the meaning of this dream?

The Rebbe explained that an almond is a metaphor for the Jewish people. Just as an almond finds itself in a shell, but from it comes out nice trees, so, too, the Jewish nation: Although externally we appear like all other nations, internally the *neshomo* bears beautiful fruit which have a good taste.

Zoreah Tzedakos, p. 140

Who is an authentic dream interpreter?

Regarding which person can interpret a dream, this is only possible by a select few, *yichidei segula*, and only at certain times.

Igros Kodesh, Volume 23, p. 214

Moving into home during chodesh Elul

I suggest you postpone your move into your new home until after the month of *Menachem-Av*. The month following, *Elul*, known as the month of *rachamim* (mercy), is an auspicious time to move to your new quarters.

Sha'arei Minhag v'Halacha, Volume 2, p. 171

It is self-understood that not only is it recommended to move into a new home during the auspicious month of *Elul*, but other months that are "*mazaldik*" are also good. This person wanted to move during the month of *Menachem-Av*, which is associated with the destruction of the *Beis HaMikdash* (holy temple). In other letters the Rebbe suggests moving in after the 15th of *Av*. There is no contradiction, because the point is not to move in when the Jewish mazal is down. Best is if one can postpone the move until the entire month of *Av* is over, but second best is to move after the 15th of *Av*.

Moving on a Tuesday

If there is no great inconvenience for you to move into your new home on Tuesday, which is the day when Hashem said twice the words "*ki tov*" ("it is good"), is most auspicious. If it is at all difficult to move on Tuesday, then you can move on any other day of the week, (except Monday and Wednesday).

Igros Kodesh, Volume 15, p. 390

There is no reason given why not to move on Monday and Wednesday. Ask your Chabad mashpia or Rav for possible reason.

Chapter 10 / Miscellaneous

Who are truly yididim u'mevinim?

Someone told the Rebbe that he followed the Rebbe's advice by consulting friends who had expertise in the proper area, but they failed to answer him.

The Rebbe said that obviously these people are not "friends that are experts," because if a person is a maven he should respond. If he is not a maven, he cannot respond. The Rebbe recommended that he find other friends who would respond.

Zoreah Tzedakos, p. 140

Happy birthday

A student mentioned to the Rebbe that his birthday was the third of Cheshvan. The Rebbe wished him "mazal tov" and told him that the third of Cheshvan is Rabbi Yisrael Rishner's yahrtzeit.

May Hashem help you in all you endeavors; however, although it is the Rishner *tzaddik's yahrtzeit*, you should remain a Lubavitcher *chasid*!

Zoreah Tzedakos, p. 140

No such a thing as "I am not a Reform, Conservative, or Orthodox Jew"

A *shliach* was prepared to mail 5000 copies of this basic message to introduce himself and the Chabad movement to the entire community. The flyer had as its headline, "I am not a Reform, Conservative or Orthodox

Jew!" Beneath the headline was a picture of the *shliach* and an explanation that a Jew is a Jew and that is at the heart of the Chabad-Lubavitch philosophy.

The *shliach* sent the flyer to the Rebbe as part of his regular report. The Rebbe responded that the headline is not appropriate because it will reawaken the old argument. It is sufficient to explain, when talking about the issue, that this is the basic philosophy of Chabad-Lubavitch, but to have it in writing is more problematic than helpful.

Memo in archives

> The Rebbe did not say to what "old argument" he was referring. Was it chasidim versus misnagdim, or was it Orthodoxy versus Reform and Conservative? However, it is clear from the overall response that the act of stating in writing, "I am not a Reform, Conservative or Orthodox Jew," is itself divisive, and gives credence to the so-called different denominations within Judaism. The general approach the Rebbe taught regarding this issue is that a Jew is a Jew, is a Jew, is a Jew! One person can be more observant of Jewish law and another less observant, but both are completely and totally Jewish regardless of what building they pray in.

Jewish unity or division

Someone asked the Rebbe whether the different practices among Jewish people will lead to an eternal division between the Jews that keep *halacha* and those who do not.

The Rebbe responded, absolutely not! The Jewish people have survived 1900 years of exile, and they will survive any and all reformation.

Zoreah Tzedakos, p. 71

Chapter 10 / Miscellaneous

Do not curse gentiles

Someone told the Rebbe that her sister was ill. She requested a *brocha* that the illness go away from her sister and enter a non-Jew.

The Rebbe asked, why does the illness have to go to someone else? Let it go deep into the earth.

Zoreah Tzedakos, p. 117

No burden for the Rebbe

Someone wrote the Rebbe the following letter:

"Your kindness accepts my ignorance.

It must be a burden to you to receive my letters. I seek direction. Some of my anxieties come from fragmentation and confusion. I am split in many directions and not accomplishing any of them well."

The Rebbe responded by circling the words "a burden" and remarked, "G-d forbid rather it is very painful that 1) you find yourself in a situation which is painful, 2) Hashem's *brocha* is temporarily being held back from enabling you to have clear direction in your life *mitzvos* without any doubts whatsoever."

The Rebbe then circled the words "split in many directions" and wrote, "It is inappropriate ('split') because you were born a Jew and that is your essence which cannot be changed. Everything else that happens to you is additional and ancillary to your essence."

Nelcha b'Urchosav, p. 215

Loneliness

A person asked the Rebbe for a *brocha* to be healthy. The person said he did not even have one person in the world upon whom to call.

The Rebbe said, "You have Hashem!"

Zoreah Tzedakos, p. 119

Leaving Israel

A person told the Rebbe he has been living in Israel 41 years, but he is not succeeding. He is thinking of leaving.

The Rebbe told him Hashem should bless him that he succeed in Israel. Not only should he not leave, but he should convince others to settle in Israel.

Zoreah Tzedakos, p. 125

No reality to "magic"

Someone wrote the Rebbe he was fearful of something happening to him because of magic. The Rebbe responded, based on the words of the Rambam, that there is no reality to magic, and that he has nothing of which to be fearful.

Nelcha b'Urchosav, p. 233

Traveling legally

Someone asked the Rebbe if he should travel to Yemen in order to build a mikva there. The Rebbe asked him if he had a visa. He said yes, they respect it very much. Is your visa legal, the Rebbe asked? He said yes. The Rebbe concluded by instructing him only to go there if he has a legal visa. Then the Rebbe gave him another dollar for tzedaka and told him to exchange it there in a legal manner.

Zoreah Tzedakos, p. 125

Olympics is avoda zora

A shliach had prepared a talk that he was going to deliver at his son's bar-mitzvah. It included a lesson to be taken from the Olympic torch. Just as the torch is which inaugurates the Olympics is passed around from city to city to symbolize the beginning of these competitive games, so, too, a Jew has to pass around the spiritual torch of Torah and mitzvos, igniting the world with Hashem's light. The Shliach sent his speech to the Rebbe. The Rebbe crossed out the entire reference to the Olympic torch and wrote:

As is known, the origin of the Olympics was literal idol-worship.

Nelcha b'Urchosav, p. 232

Holocaust memorials

In regard to your idea that a memorial for the unknown holocaust martyrs be erected in Paris, I ask forgiveness, but I do not agree with your opinion in going forward with this project.

Let us picture what the martyrs would say about this, particularly since the head of this project would be *chasidim*, but not Jewish ones, rather *chasidei umos haolom* (righteous gentiles).

(Seemingly, the person who wrote the Rebbe was involved; however, the organizers who were funding it were gentiles).

I feel the money should be spent on supporting the hundreds and thousands of living holocaust survivors who are in great need of a piece of bread physically, and more so, who need a spiritual piece of bread. The primary reason they are "starving" is because there is not enough money. Therefore, if there is a way of getting funds, the first question that rises is what it should be used to erect a memorial in the city of Paris on a large plot, so that all those walking by will remind themselves that millions of Jews were killed *al Kiddush Hashem*, or should the money be used to feed the hungry, physically or spiritually, who are thirsty to know the way of Hashem in their daily lives? I think the response to this query is self-evident.

True, there is a justification to your opinion, namely, that people will more readily contribute to a fund enabling the building of a memorial in the center of Paris than giving money to feed the poor, spiritually and physically. The latter is a standard request, not exciting, etc. However, the monument idea will be seen and known by everyone, including Jewish and non-Jewish dignitaries.

Regardless of this rationalization, it is difficult to agree with investing thousands of dollars into a stone in the earth in a corner of Paris, when tens of thousands of Jews in Eretz Yisrael and the diaspora are screaming for emergency help.

Igros Kodesh, Volume 6, p. 175

Chapter 10 / Miscellaneous

Converts

The Talmud, in tractate *Shabbos* (page 146a), states clearly that the *mazal* of non-Jews who convert was present at Mount Sinai. Also see *Chida Midbar Kedmos, Ma'amor Geirim*.

Igros Kodesh, Volume 15, p. 182

> The idea of mazal, as explained in chasidus, refers to a level of the soul which is amongst the soul's true essence. When one converts to Judaism, the "truth" is revealed. This follows in line with the Chida's explanation, as referenced by the Rebbe.

Homesick and yearning

You write that your parents miss you and yearn to live close to you. True, but parents are also willing to forego living close to their children and avoid feeling lonely if they know their children are living more comfortably further away. Ultimately parents are not happy if their child compromises his living standards because of them. Especially if this compromise goes on for months and years, the people who are making the concessions get frustrated and resent it. They feel they have given away their comforts of lifestyle. Only very few people truly feel otherwise.

Igros Kodesh, Volume 14, p. 15

Passing away with holiness

A couple had planned a celebration for the completion of the writing of a new *Sefer Torah* after *Shavous*. They planned to keep the Torah scroll in a certain *shul*.

Seemingly, they invited guests who stayed with them for the *Shavous Yom Tov* so that the guests would be able to participate in the event which was to be right after *Shavous*. During *Shavous* a woman guest passed away. The couple asked the Rebbe three things:

1. How is it possible that Hashem would allow a person to pass away when she came specifically for an event associated with a *Sefer Torah*?

2. Should they change their plans on where to keep the Torah?

3. What connection does this have to them, since it happened in their house?

The Rebbe responded to the first question:

1. It is impossible for a person who is a created being, and finite, to know all the reasons of Hashem the Creator, Who is infinite. Even to know some of His reasons is impossible. Hashem says that the only way to understand Him is by looking into Torah, which means instruction. The Torah gives a Jew the instruction as to what something means.

2. According to Torah, it is impossible for evil to come from Torah and *mitzvos* of Hashem (including from His Torah scroll). Rather, on the contrary, a worse evil was prevented because of what happened.

3. Every person has a set amount of days to live (except that through extreme positive action one is able to extend that quota and, G-d forbid, through extreme bad sins one causes a decrease in his life span quota).

4. Based on all of the above, we might say that if this woman would have not been invited to the *Sefer Torah*

celebration, she would have been elsewhere when her attack impacted her; she could have been in the street, at a non-Jew's home, or at the very least in a stranger's presence. She would not have been in the company of a doctor, a friend who is religious, and she in her final moments would not have heard words of Torah, nor seen her friends and Jewish faces. Can you imagine A) the difference between the two circumstances? B) The experiences of a person in her final moments, particularly a young, religious woman on the festival of *Shavous*?

5. Based on the words of the Baal Shem Tov, it is possible that *one* of the *true* reasons that Hashem aroused the person to donate the Torah scroll was so that the end result should be the ascent of this soul with inner peace and tranquility in a Jewish home, and in a home that is guarded by a *mezuzah*, which begins with "*Shema Yisrael, Hashem Elokeinu, Hashem Echad.*"

Response to second question:

Give the Torah to the *shul* to which you had originally planned to give it. Coincide this with the woman's *sheloshim* (thirty-day period of mourning) even if the formal ceremony associated with the Torah's arrival to the *shul* will be later.

Response to third question:

A) It seems that you and your wife have great merits in that Hashem has, without effort on your part, provided you with a very great mitzvah:

1. By making it easier for a person in her last moments of life.

2. To occupy yourselves with a *mes mitzvah* (a person who is dead) until the ambulance arrived. The importance of this mitzvah is understood from the law that the high priest on *Yom Kippur* is obligated to vacate the holy of holies, in middle of his most holy service, if there is a *mes mitzvah* to which he needs to attend.

B) Merits are associated with specific obligations among them to explain to those who raise questions about similar events that the *true* purpose of such episodes is the wondrous Divine Providence that happened.

Toras Menachem Menachem Tzion, Volume 2, p. 566

Non-Jew's fulfillment

You write about your desire to learn Torah, even though you are not Jewish. I trust you know that the Torah itself has instructions as to the approach in such a situation. Torah, which includes not only the Written Torah but also the Oral Torah (Talmud, etc.) contains parts which are to be studied by gentiles, namely, those that deal with the so-called Seven Noachide Laws, in all their ramifications and details, which are incumbent upon all human beings, both Jew and gentile. On the other hand, there are other parts of the Torah which are of no relevance to gentiles, and for various reasons gentiles should not be encouraged to take time out to study them, time that they can use to better and practical advantage by studying, practicing and promoting the said Seven Noachide Laws.

In light of the above, I suggest that you should personally discuss the matter with a competent Orthodox Rabbi, who could explain the above more fully and at the same time provide you with guidance as to how to go about your study of Torah.

I would like to add a further point, which I trust you know, that from the Torah viewpoint, there is no need whatever for a gentile to convert to Judaism in order to achieve fulfillment in accordance with the design of the Creator. On the contrary, Jews are required to discourage a would-be convert from the idea of conversion, which could also be further explained to you by the Rabbi you will consult with.

Letter in archives, dated 19th of Elul, 5745

Abusing saying "l'chayim"

Since the festival of *Shavous* is rapidly approaching and it is customary to walk to *shuls* outside of the Crown Heights neighborhood to convey words of *chasidus*, I caution all those who have been neglecting the prohibition of not drinking more than four small cups of *mashke* (alcohol) not to participate on the *tahalucha* (walk to the other communities).

People have the right and free will to do whatever they wish in their personal matters, including the drinking as much *mashke* as they want, although it is my request to do otherwise. However, in regards to my missions, such as the walks on *Shavuos* and *Simchas Torah*, and the emissaries who visit remote communities during the summer months, all who abuse the rules pertaining to minimizing the intake of *mashke* are not my *shluchim*. I ask them not to participate in these activities.

All of this applies to students, the newly married, and elders. There are some who seek excuses; however, I am not interested in any excuses and justifications. What I said is what I mean in a most down-to-earth way.

Teshura Nagel, Lag B'Omer, 5757, p. 105

Transforming "Transcendental Meditation" into Jewish Meditation

It is well known that certain oriental movements, such as "Transcendental Meditation" (T.M.), Yoga, Guru, and the like, have attracted many Jewish followers, particularly among the young generation.

Inasmuch as these movements involve certain rites and rituals, they have been rightly regarded by Rabbinic authorities as cults bordering on, and in some respects actual, *avodah zarah* (idolatry). Accordingly, Rabbinic authorities everywhere, and particularly in *Eretz Yisrael*, have ruled that these cults come under all the strictures associated with *avodah zarah*, so that also their appurtenances come under strict prohibition.

Moreover, the United States Federal Court also ruled recently that such movements, by virtue of embracing certain rites and rituals, must be classified as cultic and religious movements (Cf. Malnak v. Maharishi Mahesh Yogi, U.S.D.C. of N.J. 76-341, csp. Pp. 36-50, 78).

On the other hand, certain aspects of the said movements, which are entirely irrelevant to religious worship or practices, have a therapeutic value, particularly in the area of relieving mental stress.

Chapter 10 / Miscellaneous

It follows that if these therapeutic methods insofar as they are utterly devoid of any ritual implications would be adopted by doctors specializing in the field of mental illness, it would have a two-pronged salutary effect:

Firstly, in view of the fact that these methods are therapeutically effective, while there are, regretfully, many who could benefit from such treatment, this is a matter of healing of the highest order, since it has to do with mental illness. It would, therefore, be very wrong to deny such treatment to those who need it, when it could be given by a practicing doctor.

Secondly, and this too is not less important, since there are many Jewish sufferers who continue to avail themselves of these methods through the said cults despite the Rabbinic prohibition, it can be assumed with certainty that many of them, if not all, who are drawn to these cults by the promise of mental relief, would prefer to receive the same treatment from the medical profession if they had a choice of getting it the kosher way. It would thus be possible to save many Jews from getting involved with the said cults.

It is also known, though not widely, that there are individual doctors who practice the same or similar methods as T.M. and the like. However, it seems that these methods occupy a secondary or subordinate role in their procedures. More importantly, there is almost a complete lack of publicity regarding the application of these methods by doctors, and since the main practice of these doctors is linked with the conventional neurological and psychiatric approach, it is generally assumed that whatever success they achieve is not connected with results obtained from methods relating to T.M. and the like, results which the cults acclaim with such fanfare.

In light of the above, it is suggested and strongly urged that:

1. Appropriate action be undertaken to enlist the cooperation of a group of doctors specializing in neurology and psychiatry who would research the said methods with a view to perfecting them and adopting them in their practice on a wider scale.

2. All due publicity be given about the availability of such methods from practicing doctors.

3. This should be done most expeditiously, without waiting for this vital information to be disseminated through medical journals, where research and findings usually take a long time before they come to the attention of practicing physicians. This would all the sooner counteract the untold harm done to so many Jews who are attracted daily to the said cults, as mentioned in the opening paragraph.

In conclusion: This memo is intended for all Rabbis, doctors, and laymen who are in a position to advance the cause espoused herein, the importance of which needs no further elaboration.

Needless to say, even if one feels doubtful whether he can advance this cause, or whether the expectation warrants the effort the vital importance and urgency of saving so many souls from *avodah zarah* not only warrants but dictates every possible effort, even if there be a doubt or double doubt about achieving success. This

Chapter 10 / Miscellaneous

is certainly true when there is every reason to believe that much, indeed, can be achieved, with G-d's help and *zechus harabbim*.

Memorandum, *Teves*, 5738

I print this memorandum because, since 1978, unfortunately, the Rebbe's request has not been met. The situation with cults has become much worse in that today, 20 years later, many Jews encourage other Jews to get involve with T.M. Just last November, 1997, the New York Times had as its Sunday magazine an emphasis on unorthodox worship, which included many Jewish groups who formally offer non-Torah approaches to meditation. The Rebbe's idea that conventional doctors learn and develop a kosher meditative method would surely eliminate a great majority of Jews worshiping idolatry! We appeal to anyone reading this letter to do whatever is possible to finally implement the Rebbe's suggestion. If you or anyone you might know can help personally, financially, and communally, please call me directly.

Souvenirs from Israel

As I have remarked on similar occasions, it is customary to bring back souvenirs from the lands one visits that are characteristic of native features and products, etc. I trust, therefore, that you, too, brought back with you the right souvenir from the Holy Land, namely, an extra measure of holiness, which will serve as a fitting memento of your visit.

Letter in archives

Relating to afterlife

G-d has made it possible for human beings to grasp some aspects and insights about life and afterlife. One of these revealed truths is that the *neshomo* ia a part of G-dliness and is immortal. When the time comes for it to return to Heaven, it leaves the body and continues its eternal life in the spiritual World of Truth.

It is also a matter of common sense that, whatever the direct cause of the separation of the soul from the body (whether a fatal accident, or a fatal illness, etc.), it could affect only any of the vital organs of the physical body, but could in no way affect the spiritual soul.

A further point, which is also understandable, is that during the soul's lifetime on earth in partnership with the body, the soul is necessarily "handicapped" in certain respects by the requirements of the body (such as eating and drinking, etc.). Even a *tzaddik*, whose entire life is consecrated to Hashem, cannot escape the restraints of life in a material and physical environment. Consequently, when the time comes for the soul to return "home," it is essentially a release for it as it makes its ascent to a higher world, no longer restrained by a physical body and physical environment. Henceforth the soul is free to enjoy the spiritual bliss of being near to Hashem in the fullest measure. That is surely a comforting thought!

Letter, Tammuz, 5743

Dual realities: Life and death

It may be asked, if (death) is a "release" for the soul, why has the Torah prescribed periods of mourning, etc.? But there is really no contradiction. The Torah recognizes the natural feeling of grief that is felt by the loss of a near and dear one, whose passing leaves a void in the family, and the physical presence and contact of the

Chapter 10 / Miscellaneous

beloved one will be sorely missed. So the Torah has prescribed the proper periods of mourning to give vent to these feelings and to make it easier to regain the proper equilibrium and adjustment.

However, to allow oneself to be carried away by these feelings beyond the limits set by the Torah is a disservice to one's self and to all those around, as well as to the *neshomo* that has risen to new spiritual heights of eternal happiness. Thus, paradoxically, the overextended feeling of grief, which is due to the great love for the departed one, actually causes pain to the loved one, since the *neshomo* continues to take an interest in the dear one left behind, sees what is going on (even better than before), rejoices with him in his joys, etc.

There is one thing the departed soul can no longer do, and that is the actual fulfillment of the *mitzvos*, which can be carried out only jointly by the soul and body together in this material world. But this, too, can at least partly be overcome when those left behind do a few more *mitzvos* and good deeds in honor of, and for the benefit of, the dear *neshomo*.

Letter, *Tammuz*, 5743

The Rebbe, in the P.S. of this letter, writes as follows:

I do not know if you were aware of it when writing your letter on the 3rd of *Tammuz*. But it is significant that you wrote the letter on the anniversary of the beginning of the *geulo* of my father-in-law of saintly memory an auspicious time for *geulo* from all distractions and anxieties, to serve *Hashem* wholeheartedly and with joy.

It is interesting that the Rebbe referred to Gimmel Tammuz as a day of geulo. Therefore, what should we say now, after Gimmel Tammuz? Apparently, this signifies both geulo and release.

Daily relationship with departed soul

Thus there are these two antithetical factors: The freeing of the body from physical limitation and its elevation to a lofty world of spiritual truth, and on the other hand, the aforementioned loss and void. It is for this reason that we have two contrasting rulings in the Code of Jewish Law.

On the one hand, a fixed number of days were designated by our Sages of blessed memory in accordance with the Torah of truth, wherein mourning must be observed.

Yet at the same time one cannot emotionally overstress himself, adding additional days to the halachically stipulated time span. Moreover, those mourning must involve themselves in introspection and reflection as to why this loss and void has occurred to them. Indeed, this is the focal point of mourning. This is the reason for the self-scrutinizing fear and anxiety closely examining one's deeds and striving for *teshuva*, repentance, and self-betterment.

This has positive consequences. For there is then effected a link between those in the realm of human existence and the soul which has ascended above. For the soul exists eternally and perceives closely all that occurs with those who are near and dear. Every virtuous deed increases the soul's spiritual gladness. This is par-

Chapter 10 / Miscellaneous

ticularly so in the instance of those brought up and educated by the departed, this upbringing bringing about the aforementioned virtuous deeds. The soul has a share in these deeds, which are derived from its general influence and education of the surviving family members and others influenced and inspired by the departed.

Toras Menachem Menachem Tzion, p. 542

Explanation to unexpected passing of young child

Parents had lost a young girl on erev Pesach, 1988. They felt bad they could not observe shiva, since halacha dictates so in their particular case. They asked the Rebbe, why would Hashem not want them to observe shiva? Also, why would Hashem do this to such a young girl not allowing her to complete her mission, since she passed on before being obligated to perform mitzvos?

1. No human being can say with certainty that he knows the intent of Hashem (except a Prophet, who is instructed by Hashem to divulge the reason).

2. Whatever happens in our day and age, one should find a similarity in the past, with additional explanations for different situations.

3. Sometimes the current details explain something of the past.

4. Concerning Miriam of blessed memory, it is obvious that her passing was in a manner which Toras Emes instructs that it is forbidden to mourn her passing through the shiva ceremony. Rather, mourning her loss

is just for a few hours (from when she was buried on erev Pesach until the beginning of Pesach). The same is true for the sheloshim period.

5. All souls of our day and age come as a continuation to previous incarnations to complete what was missing before (entirely or partially).

6. Those who pass on before they are obligated to fulfill mitzvos do so because all they need to complete is several years, and therefore they live only a few years in this world. (Although these young souls are an exception to the rule, since most people's souls need to be on earth for 70, 80, or sometimes 120 years).

7. If Miriam had to fulfill the short few years to complete her previous incarnation, and immediately she enters Gan Eden, it is understood that one need not be troubled that she has been in paradise from *Pesach* on. Based on this, *Toras Emes* instructs the parents to have true joy during the Pesach festival.

8. Specifically, you, (referring to the wife who wrote the Rebbe) and your husband and children gave her much nachas, materially and spiritually, throughout all her years.

Toras Menachem Menachem Tzion, p. 568

Salt: removing the negative energy

The message of the Torah's requirement to salt every sacrifice, including one's meat, is to remove the blood from the animal-like instinct within the person. This blood of the meat is the life force of the animal, and by salting the meat and removing its blood, the animal-like power or passion is eliminated. Only then is the meat kosher and fit for human consumption.

Igros Kodesh, Volume 7, p. 270

How to get out of prison

The Alter Rebbe, in *Tanya*, teaches us that each person is in prison. This jail is the body, which takes the soul as a prisoner. The body comes from earth and will return to earth. The soul is verily a part of Hashem. So why does Hashem allow the soul to enter the body? *Chasidus* explains that the reason for this is to cause a higher elevation for the soul. This is accomplished by the soul coming into the body.

As the famous expression brought in *chasidus* says, "*yireda tzorech aliya*" ("the descent is for the purpose of the ascent"). By transforming the body and its desires, the soul attains the greatest type of elevation, something it could not have had had it not come into the body. When a person reflects on this, he realizes the reason that his G-dly soul has been relegated to living within the confines of his body. It is an advantage for him!

It is likewise true for anyone who is in prison that his purpose is to reflect about life and make good resolutions to lead a better lifestyle, thus enabling him to go free. Additionally, in jail there is no noise and tumult to disturb one as there is in free society. Therefore, even such a place as a jail has a spark of G-dly energy which sustains it, or otherwise it would become naught. This spark is the ability to think clearly and honestly about improving one's life without disturbances.

By releasing one's soul from its captivity in the body,

by understanding the purpose and goal of the imprisonment, Hashem reciprocates and actually assists one in going free from the jail term.

Sefer Hechel Menachem, Volume 3, pp. 59-61

Looking at the Rebbe's picture

She should look at a picture of my father-in-law, the saintly Rebbe (Previous Rebbe). Whenever she feels her good inclination weakening, she should remember that he, too, being a true shepherd of Israel, is looking at her at that moment. This will help her with the aforesaid problem.

Souvenir Journal, 3 Tammuz, 5757, Yeshivas Ohr Menachem, Johannesburg, South Africa, p. 78

I read a copy of this letter in the Rebbe's handwriting. The above is an English translation. The person had a problem, (which is not specified in the handwritten note) that caused her good inclination to goof off and not do what she was supposed to.

Do not avoid a Din Torah

In regard to the dispute you have with so-and-so, I have already told him that he has no right to avoid a *Din Torah*. I hope that both of you will go to a *beis din* to work it out.

Sefer Hechel Menachem, Volume 3, p. 64

I do not take responsibility for what is said in my name

It is public knowledge that I write down with my

own handwriting my responses (or I say the responses at public farbrengens).

Sefer Hechel Menachem, Volume 3, p. 66

There are no "misnagdim" today

You write about the known *misnaged*. I must inform you that today there are no true *misnagdim* as there were in the olden days, since that opposition to *chasidus* was based on certain suspicions, as history attests, too.

Since those days it has been proven time and again that the concerns were not justified. Therefore, today, one who is in opposition to *chasidus* either does not know the entire historical event and its abolition, or simply does not care to know the facts. This way he is able to fight the chasidic movement for reasons that are not based on holiness.

Sefer Hechel Menachem, Volume 3, p. 72

Say Tefilas HaDerech daily during a trip

I inform you of my father-in-law's conduct when he took trips, leaving his home for several months at a time, that although he stayed in one place on his trip, he said the prayer for traveling known as *Tefilas Haderech* each day after his morning davening. He would say it without mentioning Hashem's name at the end in the *brocha*.

Igros Kodesh, Volume 20, p. 82

Safety measures for car trips

You write about their car trip. In addition to taking along their *tefillin*, each one traveling should also take along a book of *Tehillim* and *Tanya*. During the trip, let them study at least several lines from the *Tanya* and say several chapters of *Tehillim*.

Igros Kodesh, Volume 19, p. 268

Doing mivtzoim on trips

In addition to *Tefilas Haderech* as a protective measure when traveling, let them reach out to other Jews and help them come closer to Hashem.

Sharei Halacha u'Minhag, Volume 1, p. 224

This note was written to the administrators of a girls' school who informed the Rebbe that the students were going on their annual class trip.

Shabbos entrance tickets

It is not at all acceptable to distribute tickets as a means of allowing one to enter *shul* on *Shabbos*, for reasons associated with *chilul Hashem*, *maris ayin* (wrong appearance to an outsider), and what people will say.

Likutei Sichos, Volume 24, p. 343

This letter was written in 1943, when some shuls had the practice of requiring tickets in order to gain entry on certain Shabbosos when there was a famous cantor leading the davening. The Rebbe feels that although the shul distributed the tickets in a permissible manner, people who are not familiar with the practice might say that the tickets were bought on Shabbos or something else that would be a chilul Hashem.

Swimming

The Rebbe points out that it is human nature to be social, each person to a different degree. It is as if you're standing on the edge of a pool and are contemplating swimming, but you don't know how to swim: If you remain on the outside of the pool, you'll never learn how to swim. The only way you learn is by jumping in. So it is with removing loneliness and depression. One must begin by "jumping in" to a circle of people, and then one will eventually benefit from that first forceful step.

Igros Kodesh, Volume 18, p. 534

This letter was written to a woman who was suffering from depression and loneliness. The lesson one can take from swimming is the importance of getting involved with other people and not to be a loner. Swimming teaches that it can only happen if you simply jump in.

Charms, amulets

Regarding your question about the validity of amulets, I have not heard anything at all about these issues.

Igros Kodesh, Volume 20, p. 119

EPILOGUE

After reading 125 pages of advice on day-to-day issues, one must ask the big questions. Am I willing to follow? Why should I adhere? To whom am I listening? The response to these questions depends on whom you really are. According to a Jewish saying, you write like you talk, you talk like you feel, you feel like you think, and you think like you are.

Who are you? A Jew knows that he or she is an inherently joyful subject of G-d. A Jew knows that, as a servant of G-d, the only reality is His Torah. A Jew, as a subject of G-d whose reality is Torah, knows that there are *tzaddikim*, righteous individuals in each generation who were planted to manifest and communicate G-d's will regarding Torah.

In order for one to activate his relationship with these *tzaddikim*, one must act according to the last word in the *Shema*, which is "Echad." In the Hebrew language, this word is spelled with the three letters *alef*, *cheis*, and *daled*. *Alef* stands for the word "*ohr*" ("light") *cheis* stands for the word "*chayos*" ("life"), and *daled* stands for the word "*dibur*" ("speech").

In order to talk about anything, one must first be illuminated by knowing the information (light). Gathering the data is a prerequisite to proper feelings. Feelings bring *chayos* (life, enthusiasm, excitement, and warmth). Finally, once one has the data, which inspires proper healthy feelings, he can speak about these feelings (speech).

In order to truly and fully appreciate the advice, one needs to learn the Torah of the *tzaddik*. Once that has been accomplished, one proceeds to feeling close to the *tzaddik*, bonding himself to the *tzaddik*. When one understands and feels what this *tzaddik* is all about, on an intellectual and emotional level, one culminates the relationship by speaking and following the *tzaddik's* words. At this point in the relationship, there is a true harmony of mind, heart, and action.

Can one come to a deep, true attachment with the *tzaddik* without the above criteria? Yes, it is possible. However, that is the exception to the rule. The norm is to study, feel, and act.

I say to all the readers, regardless of whether or not you saw or knew the Rebbe, you can develop a relationship with him. This is just as true now, after his passing, as before in fact, maybe more so, because the previous restrictions, limitations, and requirements no longer apply after the *tzaddik* leaves the world (see *Tanya, Igeres HaKodesh*, chapter 27). However, for his advice to be effective, there are several suggestions to follow (not in chronological order):

1. Believe in this *tzaddik* as someone who is completely permeated by G-d and Torah.

Epilogue

2. Be willing to accept what he advises, regardless of your opinion.

3. Study his teachings, talks, discourses, and letters.

4. Implement his *mitzvah* campaigns, including the following: a) learning topics about Moshiach and doing deeds to bring Moshiach, b) loving every Jew, c) providing a Jewish education for each child, d) daily Torah study, e) *tefillin*, f) *mezuzah*, g) *tzedaka*, h) having a house full of Jewish books, h) family purity, i) women and girls lighting *Shabbos* candles, j) keeping kosher, k) learning Rambam daily, and l) teaching non-Jews their seven Noachide laws.

5. Remember that the advice is general; for it to be adapted specifically to your personal life, consult an expert Chabad-Lubavitch *chasid* who has the proper experience. The *chasid* has a relationship with the Rebbe that makes him or her the appropriate person you can trust to guide you in the right direction.

May G-d help us all to be reunited with our holy Rebbe, through the coming of our righteous Moshiach now! Then there will be no need to ask each other for guidance and assistance, since we will all hear and see our Rebbe and all other *tzaddikim* who will walk hand in hand with Moshiach. All problems will disappear, and we will be focused on going from good to better. Amen; may it be now!

Glossary

Glossary

Ahavas Yisroel: loving one's fellow Jew

Alter Rebbe (lit., "the Old Rebbe"): Rabbi Schneur Zalman of Liadi (1745-1812), the founder of the Chabad-Lubavitch trend within the chasidic movement; author of the Tanya, a classic text of the chasidic tradition, and of the Shulchan Aruch HaRav, a classic legal code

Amida: the "standing service"; also known as the silent prayer. It is the central part of the prayer service, also called the "Shemoneh Esreh" (the "Eighteen" Blessings)

Arizal (lit., "the lion of blessed memory"): acronym for R. Isaac Luria (1534-1572), one of the leading luminaries of the kabbalah

Baal Shem Tov (lit., "Master of the Good Name"): Rabbi Yisrael ben Eliezer (1698-1760), founder of the chasidic movement

Beis HaMikdash: the (first, second, or third) Temple in Jerusalem

Chabad (acronym for the Hebrew words meaning "wisdom, understanding, and knowledge"): the approach to chasidism which filters its spiritual and emotional power through the intellect; a synonym for the Chabad movement is Lubavitch, the name of the town where this movement originally flourished

Challah: The mitzvah of seperating a piece of dough when baking.

Chasid (pl. chasidim): a pious person; specifically, the term is used to refer to a follower of a chasidic holy man (Rebbe, tzaddik) and a member of the chasidic movement of the Baal Shem Tov

Chasidus, Chasidism: the study of the Torah's inner meaning, also known as Jewish mysticism

Chazon: cantor

Glossary

Chinuch: lit. "dedication" or "education"

Cheder (pl., chadarim): school in which young children learn reading skills and begin the study of Torah

Chumash (pl., chumashim): five books of Moses. See Torah.

Emes: truth

Emuna: faith

Eretz Yisroel: the land of Israel

Erev: Eve. Generally used for the daylight hours before a holy day, as for example, "erev Shabbos"

Gaon: a title denoting exceptional rabbinic learning and genius

Gehenom: Purgatory/Hell

Halacha (pl., halachos): (a) the body of Torah law; (b) a particular law

Hashem: literally, "The Name" (the four-letter Name of G-d that cannot be uttered); this is a way of referring to G-d

Havdalah: the religious ceremony at the end of Shabbos and holidays

Kabbalah (lit., "received tradition"): the Jewish mystical tradition

Kabbalas ol (lit., "the acceptance of G-d's yoke"): an unwaivering, selfless commitment to doing the will of G-d

Kashrus: the kosher laws

Kiddush: Shabbos and holiday ceremonial service performed over wine, commonly observed Friday night

Ma'amar: a formal chasidic discourse

Matza Shmura: hand-baked matza, with greatest halachic care taken in its baking

Mesiras Nefesh (lit., sacrifice of the soul"): the willingness to sacrifice oneself, either through martyrdom or through a selfless life, for the sake of the Torah and its commandments

Mezuzah: writing of the Shema on piece of parchment, placed on all door posts

Midrash: classical collection of the sages, homiletic teachings on the Torah

Mikva: a ritual bath used by women for purification after

The Rebbe's Advice

    emerging from the state of niddah (spiritual impurity) and used by both men and women in their endeavors to attain spiritual self-refinement

Mincha: the daily afternoon prayer service

Minyon: the minimum prayer quorum of ten

Mishne: ancient collection of legal decisions of the sages; the earliest part and core of the Talmud

Moshiach: lit., "the anointed one"; the Messiah

Motzoei (lit., "the going out of"): the night after a Shabbos or festival

Moshe Rabbeinu (lit., "Moses our teacher"): the "father of the prophets," who redeemed the Jews from Egypt and brought them to the revelation at Mount Sinai

Ohel: (literally "tent,") refers to the graveside of the Rebbe and previous Rebbe

Parshah: the Torah portion for any particular Shabbos or festive occasion

Previous Rebbe: Rabbi Yosef Yitzchok Schneerson (1880-1950), the sixth Rebbe of Chabad-Lubavitch

Rabeinu Tam's tefillin: tefillin with the four Torah portions arranged in the order prescribed by Rabbi Tam (1100-1171)

Reb: a title of respect; Mister

Rambam (acronym for Rabbi Moshe ben Maimon, 1135-1204): Maimononides, one of the foremost Jewish thinkers of the Middle Ages; wrote the Mishneh Torah, Guide for the Perplexed, etc.

Rashi (acronym for Rabbi Shlomo Yitzchaki, 1040-1105): the author of the foremost commentary to the Torah and the Talmud

Rebbe (lit., "my teacher [or master]"): saintly Torah leader who serves as spiritual guide to chasidim

Rosh haYeshiva: Dean of a yeshiva (lit., "sitting," referring to an academy of Torah studies, in which one of the principal methods of learning is dialogue between students to discover the meaning of the teachers, lectures and the underlying texts.)

Rov: ordained rabbi who makes halachic rulings

Glossary

Shabbos: the Sabbath

Shidduch (pl, shidduchim): proposed mate, believed to be heaven-sent, commonly called "bashert"

Shulchan Aruch: the standard Code of Jewish law compiled by Rabbi Yosef Caro in the mid-sixteenth century

Sivan: the third month of the Jewish year

Talmid (pl. Talmidim): disciple, student

Talmud: the sixty volumes of Jewish law, expounding upon the Torah. It is comprised of the Mishne and the (later) discussion and commentary called the Gemara. The terms Talmud and Gemara are used interchangeably

Tanach: see Torah

Tanya: the classic text of Chabad chasidic thought, authored by Rabbi Schneur Zalman of Liadi (the Alter Rebbe)

Tefillin: two small leather boxes, each containing four Torah passages, worn daily by adult Jewish males during the morning prayers

Tehillim (lit., "praises"): the Book of Psalms, authored by King Dovid

Teshuva (lit., "return [to G-d]"): repentance

Tikun (pl. tikunim): corrective measure(s) to atone for transgressing G-d's will

Torah: the five books of Moshe; the Tanach [acronym for Torah, Naviim, and Kesuvim; that is, the five books of Moshe, plus the Prophets and the (Holy) Writings]; or, more broadly, all Jewish writings throughout the ages. See also Chumash.

Tzaddik (pl. tzaddikim): a righteous or holy person; leader of a chasidic group, a Rebbe

Tzedaka: charity

Yeshiva: Rabbinical academy

Yetzer Hara: evil inclination

Yetzer Tov: good inclination

Yechidus: private audience with the Rebbe

Zohar: the "Book of Splendor," the central book of the kabbalah, the Jewish mystical tradition, authored by Rabbi Shimon Bar Yochai (2nd century)